Camp Gramma

Camp Gramma

Putting Down Spiritual Stakes For Your Grandchildren

Judi Braddy

BEACON HILL PRESS
OF KANSAS CITY

Copyright 2009
by Judi Braddy and Beacon Hill Press of Kansas City

ISBN 978-0-8341-2373-1

Cover Design: J.R. Caines
Internal Design: Sharon Page

All Scripture quotations not otherwise designated are from the *Holy Bible, New International Version*® (NIV®). Copyright © 1973, 1978, 1984 by International Bible Society. Used by permission of Zondervan Publishing House. All rights reserved.

Permission to quote from the following additional copyrighted versions of the Bible is acknowledged with appreciation:

The *New American Standard Bible*® (NASB®), © copyright The Lockman Foundation 1960, 1962, 1963, 1968, 1971, 1972, 1973, 1975, 1977, 1995.

The *Holy Bible, Today's New International Version*® (TNIV)®. Copyright © 2001, 2005 by International Bible Society®. Used by permission of International Bible Society®. All rights reserved worldwide.

Library of Congress Cataloging-in-Publication Data

Braddy, Judi, 1948-
   Camp Gramma : putting down spiritual stakes for your grandchildren / Judi Braddy.
     p. cm.
   Includes bibliographical references.
   ISBN 978-0-8341-2373-1 (pbk.)
   1. Christian education—Home training. 2. Grandparent and child—Religious aspects—Christianity. 3. Grandmothers—Religious life. I. Title.
   BV1590.B73 2009
   248.8'45—dc22

2009012944

Dedicated to my six grandest grands!

Fallon Michael Forrest Braddy
Liam James Braddy
McKayla Sloan Braddy
Olivia Roseanne Braddy
Logan James Braddy
Kayla Rose Andreachi

I love you more'n anything!

Contents

Acknowledgments		9
1.	Let the Games Begin!	11
	Camp Gramma Clipboard #1	
2.	Staking Out Our Territory	23
	Camp Gramma Clipboard #2	
3.	Sleeping Bags	37
	Camp Gramma Clipboard #3	
4.	Around the Old Campfire	49
	Camp Gramma Clipboard #4	
5.	May I Have S'mores, Please?	65
	Camp Gramma Clipboard #5	
6.	Blazing a Trail	83
	Camp Gramma Clipboard #6	
7.	Over the River and Through the Woods	99
	Camp Gramma Clipboard #7	
8.	Survival Skills	115
	Camp Gramma Clipboard #8	
9.	Leaving a Light On	133
	Camp Gramma Clipboard #9	
10.	Bug Spray	145
	Camp Gramma Clipboard #10	
11.	Breaking Camp	161
	Camp Gramma Clipboard #11	
12.	Roots and Wings	175
	Camp Gramma Clipboard #12	
Notes		187

Acknowledgments

Camp Gramma Kudos to
Jim, my husband and campsite companion. You're a fabulous dad, world's greatest grampa, and a real trooper—even when I'm not a happy camper.

Damon, Derek, and Dustin, my three sons. Your personal reflections warmed my heart and brought tears to my eyes—not to mention that two of you have produced five of the world's most gorgeous and intelligent grandchildren.

James, my big brother. You blazed the trail before me and provided some delightfully surprising family perspectives.

All the grandmas who shared their hearts. Like crackle logs, your colorful stories made the book pop.

Bonnie and Judi, my fabulous and unflappable editors. You stuck with me even when I needed "s'more" time.

Barry, Jen, Teresa, Lynda, and all the Beacon Hill staff. Like marshmallows and chocolate on the graham crackers of life, you serve your authors and others so sweetly and always have us covered.

Jan, Craig, and Diane. Your cozy cabins provided me the perfect place to cocoon and put words on paper. You, my friends, truly served as sleeping bags on the rocky soil of my life, writing and otherwise.

And most important of all, thank you, God, for assigning me life's most amazing opportunity and privilege: being a wife, mom, and gramma.

Let the Games Begin!

> *Children's children are a crown to the aged,
> and parents are the pride of their children.*
> —Proverbs 17:6

When first learning that my husband and I were going to be grandparents, I had four words to say:

"Let the games begin!"

I love being a grandma. To my way of thinking, it's maximum fun with minimum responsibility. Yesiree! Gramma's my name—spoiling is my game. Imagine my shock to learn that some people take a bit more convincing.

Why? For one thing, it seems becoming a grandparent is unavoidably associated with aging. After all, the right of passage to grandparentdom is that you must first have children of your own. Or, as a dear friend of mine so sweetly expressed it, "Becoming a grandparent is your reward for not killing your own children."

Even so, some of us are just not ready. We simply don't see ourselves as old, and in many cases we're not. Fact is, thanks to the miracles of modern medicine, hair color, and cosmetics, grandparents seem to be getting younger all the time. Even those a little farther down the road when the grands join the entourage often don't feel it or look it.

I can identify. If, as they now say, 40 is the new 30, then being only 45 when our first grandson was born, I barely met the criteria. To me that was—and still is—part of the fun. I love it when people say, "Why, you don't look old enough to be a grandmother!" Even if they're just being nice, it's music to my egotistical ears.

The reality is that some of us are even young enough to still have a teenager or two at home. The last thing we want is to take on another toddler, even in small doses—or worse, end up raising our children's children, something that's happening more and more in this generation.

The majority of us, however, have arrived at the stage of life where we're finally embracing the freedom of the empty nest. We've managed to get all our own kids out of the house and are living somewhat independently when—boom! We get the *big announcement*. How fair is that? Our affections, not to mention our pocketbooks, are again in danger of being compromised. It gives the term *baby boomers* a whole new meaning.

So what's a potentially begrudging grandparent to do? Here's a suggestion: lighten up! I'm here to tell you that even under less-than-desirable circumstances, this generation of grandparenting can be a glorious new game.

Consider one common way we combat the conflict and forestall the stereotype: the name game. Now instead of, as the old song goes, "over the river and through the woods to Grandmother's house we go," it's "over the freeway and through the subdivision to Nana's, Mimi's, or Grammy's condo." And Grampa isn't Grampa anymore. He's Poppie, Papa, or, as our oldest granddaughter dubbed my husband when she was tiny, Poopah.

Judging from a recent e-mail I received from "akamima"—also known as Mima—these are names we wear like badges of honor, even incorporate into our e-mail addresses. What we're saying to the world is "Sure, I may be a grandma, but I'm no ordinary grandma—I'm a groovin' granny." My friend Sharon Hoffman's newest book is titled *A Car Seat in My Convertible?* That says it all![1]

Simply put, we're not your grandma's grandma.

Come to think of it, maybe that's why some grandparents go conversely crazy. They're out to prove that having grandchildren is *not* going to change their image, lifestyle, or outlook all that much. Consider the following anonymous poem I recently ran across.

> *In the dim and distant past*
> *When life's tempo wasn't fast,*
> *Gramma used to rock and knit*
> *Crochet and tat and babysit.*
> *Gramma now is at the gym,*
> *Exercising to keep slim,*
> *Now she's golfing with the bunch,*
> *Taking clients out to lunch.*
> *Going north to ski and curl,*
> *And all her days are in a whirl.*
> *Nothing seems to stop or block her*
> *Now that Gramma's off her rocker.*[2]

Trying to avoid any such embarrassing accusation, my husband and I settled quite happily into the standard sobriquets of Gramma and Grampa. Truth is, we don't care what our grandkids call us—as long as they call us often. The only thing I don't want to be dubbed is "Grouch"—though on our first family trip to Disneyland we purchased a baseball hat for my husband with an embroidered, labeled picture of Grumpy, the dwarf of the *Snow White* saga. There are reasons for that, however, having nothing exclusively to do with being a grandfather—or with this illustration, for that matter. This is merely my stream-of-consciousness stab at him for once considering it clever to announce publicly his difficult adjustment to living with a grandma.

But I digress.

In the great scheme of things, any name is infinitely better than being called Big Mama or Big Papa, as a childhood friend of mine called her grandparents. If memory serves, they were originally from Texas. Maybe everything is bigger and better there, but somehow the mental image I got of giant-sized grandparents still seems a little scary to me. All that is to say that whatever name we choose to use, let's keep things in proper proportion.

Perhaps the biggest issue for some is that we can't believe our children are ready to be parents. It's that whole *Fiddler on the Roof* "Sunrise, sunset—quickly go the years" thing. Suddenly our babies are all grown up and having babies of their own. Where did the time go? Talk about a reality (mortality?) check. Not only are we not ready—it's hard to imagine that *they* can possibly be.

Face it—no matter how old our children get, somehow they never seem sufficiently mature in our eyes to mother or father children of their own. And many aren't.

But then again, were *we*?

I'll be the first to admit that raising my own children was not necessarily the wonderful, heartwarming experience others describe. Don't get me wrong—we had some great times and made wonderful memories. Still, looking back now, I see how ill-equipped I really was.

Being raised basically as an only child—my brother was 14 years older—gave me no practical experience in dealing with children, siblings or otherwise. On top of that, I was 18—barely more than a child myself—when I married my handsome minister husband. We then proceeded to have three babies in less than five years, all boys who were "all boy." I had no clue how to handle them.

Nor did I have much outside help. For most of our children's formative years, ministry assignments moved us hundreds of miles from either of our Midwest-rooted parents. Though I talked often to my parents by phone, it wasn't the same as living nearby, where I could occasionally dump—oh, I mean *ask* them to take—the kids for a while so I could have a much-needed break. Thank goodness for a few faithful baby-sitters.

To complicate matters further, living on a pastor's meager salary often necessitated my working outside the home, creating that now-more-common-than-ever juggling act between church, career, and family. How I ever kept all the plates spinning, parental or otherwise, I don't know. Admittedly there were many things I would have and should have done differently. Somehow, though, we managed to raise our children without irreparably maiming or mistreating them. The choices they made after that were their own.

This brings me to another great thing about being a grandparent. It's like getting a do-over—a second chance at doing things right. Having learned from our own parenting mistakes, we now have experience that gives us more patience and better perspective. As Job, that biblical epitome of both, rhetorically puts it, "Is not wisdom found among the aged? Does not long life bring understanding?" (Job 12:12).

One would hope.

Surely, having been around the block more than once, we at least have a greater grasp on the time required for lessons to take root and grow. Hindsight helps us see the big picture rather than the isolated episodes we experienced with our own children. As a result, the anxiety and urgency we felt with them have dissipated somewhat.

Also, since grandparents don't have to be the main disciplinarians, we can offer objectivity—something that parents, due to close proximity, often can't. Best of all, when the grandkids get grumpy, we can send them home.

The bottom line is this: ready or not, here the grandchildren come. And once they start coming, the parents often don't seem to know how to make it stop. Starting with that first tow-headed heart-tugger, we welcomed three grandchildren in less than three years. To date, we have five biological grandbabies and a sixth by serendipitous assimilation. If our youngest, still-single son gets with the program, we could have more. I often wonder if he's postponing marriage on purpose after having made certain astute observations.

Truth is, once the grandkids come along, our kids are pretty much on their own. As my middle son once lamented, "Sometimes I think all you care about is seeing the grandkids. It's like we don't even count anymore."

Hey—he had his chance.

And he might be right. Why else do we suddenly find ourselves running all over town trying to find just the right princess bed or pirate booty, even fighting off other parents or grandparents for the last most-in-demand toy or video game on the shelf? Besides the sheer joy of seeing their little faces light up, we want them to care about seeing us too. If that requires bribery, so be it.

This brings me to the greatest grandparenting news of all: it can be *fun*!

That's why, a few years ago, anticipating a week's vacation with the four oldest grands, I spent days transforming our backyard into a summer camp complete with tent, cots, and sleeping bags. The barbeque became a campfire for cooking burgers, dogs, and s'mores. From Build-a-Bear to bowling, daily activities and outings were painstakingly planned. The hand-painted sign tacked on the gazebo said it all: CAMP GRAMMA.

When the long-awaited moment finally came, Grumpy, er, Grampa and I excitedly welcomed their arrival with smiles and hugs, then eagerly took them on the grand tour of all we had constructed. In and out of the tent they crawled. Off and onto the cots they bounced. With all the hilarity we had hoped for, they embraced their required rations for the week, which included handmade fleece blankets and pillowcases and, thanks to a fabulous gift shop find, grizzly bear slippers. I had spared no expense. It was going to be a great time.

So imagine my surprise that first evening to find them all camped out in front of the TV set, four pairs of grizzly bear slippers protruding at odd angles from wall-to-wall sleeping bags.

"How come you guys aren't out in the tent?"

"We like it in here," chirped the oldest.

"It-th dark and th-cary out there," lisped the youngest.

"Nonsense. Grampa promised he'd sleep outside. Say—where *is* Grampa?"

As if on cue, a loud snore erupted from a large, blanketed lump nearby.

Deserter.

"Okay," I conceded with a sigh. "Let's hit the hay. Tomorrow's gonna be busy."

"Gramma"—a sleepy voice drifted from the bunched-up bedding—"will you tell us a Bible story?"

"And don't forget to remember our prayers," called another contented camper.

How could I "forget to remember"? It had been our bedtime routine for every previous visit. Hmmm. Maybe I had gotten a bit too caught up in this new camping crusade.

Later, as I watched them sleep, a warm truth snuggled its way in. Being a Christian grandparent is a bit more than just fun and games, after all. It includes not only instilling self-confidence and providing a safe place when the world gets dark and "th-cary," but also driving down those all-important spiritual stakes as well. Quite simply, it serves as both an earthly and eternal assignment.

How important it is that, amid all the love and laughter, we also understand the weightiness of weaving heredity into legacy! For our children and grandchildren we provide a link to the past, an anchor in the present, and a passport to the future. That's why the choices we make in how we handle this new phase of life are so significant. As author Amy Tan put it, "If you can't change your circumstances, change your attitude."

For me, it meant making this determination: I will do whatever I can to remain an important part of my grandchildren's lives in hopes of making things better for them and their parents, not only financially but also emotionally and spiritually. How grateful I am to God that at my "ripe old age" I still have the health and energy to do that!

Guess this brings us full circle to that growing-old thing again. Considering the alternative, though, especially as it's related to wisdom and understanding, age isn't such a bad thing. So grow up, Grandma, and deal with it.

How do you do that? I'm glad you asked, for therein lies one of life's greatest adventures, one that we'll explore together in the following pages.

Certainly grandparenting has changed considerably over the years. What hasn't changed is that no matter how far away they wander, our own kids will eventually settle down and wind their way back home. We shouldn't be surprised, when they do, that one child or more soon comes trailing after them. As Grandma and Grandpa—or whatever we choose to call ourselves—we must anticipate their arrival by making a place not only in our homes but also in our hearts. As Martha Stewart would say, "It's a good thing."

More important than Martha is the promise found in Proverbs 14:26: "He who fears the LORD has a secure fortress, and for his children it will be a refuge"—and, I might add, for their children too.

A fortress and refuge—that's Camp Gramma, where memories are made not only for a lifetime but also for eternity.

Let the games begin.

CAMP GRAMMA CLIPBOARD #1

Ready to tackle your own Camp Gramma? Here are a few tips from me and other experienced folks you'll meet later in the book.

- Martha Bolton's basic "Camp Nana" goes like this. She finds Vacation Bible School supplies at local craft or Christian book stores and buys as many of the fun projects as she can. Then, during summer vacation, she has all the grandkids over to make crafts and share the coordinating Bible story. Not only do they learn something and have fun, but it also gives them souvenirs to take home from Nana's.
- Should you decide to plan something a little more elaborate, remember that balance is still the key. You want to keep the kids from getting bored but not have them totally tuckered out by the end of the day. Or maybe you *do*.
- Setting a budget beforehand helps you decide how all-out you can afford to go. Most visits should probably involve only small-scale activities, saving the major theme park or faraway outings for special years. Either way, planning ahead allows you to save up or collect materials and fun stuff over a period of time, avoiding one big outlay of expense. This is especially important if not everyone lives locally and travel is involved.
- Stuck on a theme? Start by checking out Christian supply stores, catalogs, and web sites to see what Vacation Bible School lesson materials are being offered. Order only what you need to teach or illustrate the lesson, keeping in mind that you can often find coordinating clothing, crafts, toys, stickers, and so on at discount stores. Dollar stores and party places are good resources, as well as online companies like <www.orientaltrading.com>.

- Ann Gibson suggests starting when the children are a little older. In hindsight, age three is a bit too young for taking trips and for five- or six-day stays. "Or," she says, "you could start with fewer days then add on." Also take into consideration the ages and abilities of your campers when choosing activities and teaching materials.
- Another suggestion from Ann is to plan one service project for the week. It's a great way to get your campers thinking outside the flaps. Connie Clements solved the too-young trauma by doing a one-day preschool camp for the three-year-olds as soon as their siblings went back to school. The promise of this made it a little easier for them to say goodbye when the older kids left for Camp Gramma.
- My time-tested schedule is to have a leisurely breakfast, followed by the Bible lesson and accompanying games, craft, or workbook while they're still alert. If weather permits, we often do this outside on the patio table. Some type of outing or special activity is planned in the afternoon. The rest of the time can be filled in with whatever they like to do. A daily highlight is getting to choose one item from the "treasure trunk" I keep stuffed with toys and games. Usually this is something interactive.
- In case you still need specific theme ideas to get you going, some I've used are *Summer of the Monkeys, Summer of the Pirates,* and *Summer of the Spies.* The last two were based around Vacation Bible School themes I found online. It was easy and so much fun to find hats, stickers, bookmarks, and other related paraphernalia. For the *Spies* theme, each child got a bright plastic portfolio folder with everything needed to be Bible detectives—badges, magnifying glasses, notepads, pens, flashlights, and so on. For fun, I even came across crime scene tape and plastic "Uzis" that shot silly string. A *huge* hit!

- Bottom line: Don't be so locked into anything that your time together becomes stressful. The point is to make memories, not ulcers. Try to end each day with some type of relaxing spiritual reflection.

Now—put up the tents, pull out the stops, and start driving down those spiritual stakes!

2
Staking Out Our Territory

> LORD, *you have assigned me my portion and my cup; you have made my lot secure. The boundary lines have fallen for me in pleasant places; surely I have a delightful inheritance.*
> —Psalm 16:5-6

Camped out at the hospital when it was time for our first grandson to be born, we received another rude awakening. In addition to our son and daughter-in-law, two other people turned up to wait out the long hours of labor. Suddenly the adjustment of becoming grandparents gave way to another overriding truth: we weren't the only grandparents present here. The competition for "Best Grandma and Grandpa" had officially begun, and only one thing mattered.

We had to win.

I'm kidding, of course—I think. Okay, maybe we can't completely escape a little reined-in rivalry, but in the great game of grandparenting there's really no need for serious campsite competition. Each of us has a place and provides a perspective in our grandchildren's lives.

Take for instance our daughter-in-law Deirdra's mother, who was born and raised in Chile. She now lives in a tiny apartment in San Francisco where, having no car, she commutes everywhere by public transit. Her South American insights make for some very interesting visits and discussions, as do the periodic excursions our grands make into the city where she delights in taking them to her favorite out-of-the-way places. Undoubtedly her eclectic cultural influence provides a varied and interesting view of the world.

Our other grandchildren's maternal grandmother comes from a fairly large family, including two siblings who inherited a recessive gene causing dwarfism. This resulted in a number of related physical problems. As well, their same-side grandfather suffered most of his adult life with the debilitating disease of multiple sclerosis. Certainly it was sad watching their ongoing health issues, yet we've also seen the grandchildren develop an early acceptance and compassion for people who are different or deal with physical handicaps. Much, I'm convinced, is due to their maternal grandmother's compassionate, keep-going model.

Undoubtedly there are times as we stake out our grandparenting territory when we, too, must learn to deal magnanimously and diplomatically with extended family. My friend Arlene Allen tells of going to visit her then-four-year-old grandson, Grant. One day as the family was gathered, he unexpectedly announced, "Grandma, you're the best grandma I have." With her daughter-in-law sitting right there, Arlene felt a bit embarrassed. She quickly composed a politically correct response.

"Thank you, Grant, but remember you have another grandma. I'm sure there are things about both of us that you really like." This, her grandson fairly and readily agreed, was true.

Still, the minute the boy and his mom made their exit, Arlene couldn't resist the temptation. Looking at her husband, she gave the old one-arm pump along with a soft victory shout, "Yes!" For this visit anyway, she got to hold the trophy.

It's tricky business becoming a grandparent. For first-timers in particular, it may take a while to figure out exactly where we fit in. My experience reveals that this is especially true when it's your son's children rather than your daughter's. As the mother of three sons, I soon discovered that in the deck of life, daughters-in-law often hold the upper hand. Thankfully, I've been blessed with wonderful ones who even under less-than-desirable circumstances have embraced us as an integral part of our grandchildren's lives. Any reader struggling with an in-law relationship will hopefully find in the following pages some helpful hints for garnering good will, repairing rifts, and avoiding territorial trip-ups.

Often this depends on how close we are in proximity. Naturally grandparents who live nearby have more frequent hands-on input—and opportunities for interference—than those who live farther away. We are the ones whose help is most likely to be solicited, and usually we're quick to pitch in. Not only do we serve as frequent baby-sitters but also as chauffeurs and homework helpers. We can also be seen sitting on the sidelines of varied and voluminous sports activities, not to mention getting pegged for dropping off and picking up from practices. As a result, they can come to depend on us—sometimes too much.

My ultra-organized friend Peggy Musgrove is one such grandma who delights in helping her two working daughters by frequently watching and transporting their children. Her 13-year-old grandson even has the habit of sometimes showing up at her house after school to get a snack, spend some time "talking" via computer to his friends, then to do homework until his parents come home from work.

Recently back-to-back conferences caused Peggy and her husband to be gone for an unusually extended length of time, relegating the grandson to spending time at home alone with his brother. On one particularly difficult day, he gloomily asked his mom when Grandma and Grandpa would be home. Upon discovering it would still be a few more days, he let out a loud lament. "Oh, man! My life goes so much better when Grandma is around."

Could it be that some grandparents are too good at what they do? Still, her heart was so touched upon hearing this that

Peggy determined she would try not to take any more lengthy trips until the kid was grown.

For those relegated to being a long-distance grandparent, don't despair. Your influence and affection can be equally effective, a subject that will be elaborated on in a later chapter.

What is it that makes grandparents such special people? Let's talk for a moment about the term *grandparent*—or as they are called in a few other cultures, *granmere, granpere, grossmuter, grosspater, oma, opa,* and the list goes on. Wherever in the world you find them, these are people who, though one step removed from your own parents, still deserve respect and carry authority. Why? Regardless of culture, somewhere in the translation most have become better at it than we were at being parents.

First we were mere parents—now we're *grand*parents. Get it? With years of experience under our belts, we've survived the trial run and learned a thing or two about raising children. In fact, our children are sometimes amazed at how much we've learned, so much so that they now feel they can actually trust us—who knew so little when they were teenagers—with their own children's welfare.

Speaking of which, could it be that our delight in being *grand*parents springs from some slightly sinister motivation on our part—like, say, payback? There's probably not a parent alive who hasn't at some point when his or her own children were resisting rules or arguing his or her authority said these words: "I can hardly wait until you have children of your own!" Truly, to quote another homespun speck of wisdom, "You never pay for your own raisin' until you have children." No wonder we find some small satisfaction when our time finally comes to see 'em squirm.

In all fairness, despite some false starts and questionable choices, I've been amazed at what good parents our children have become. Whereas I can count on one finger (you heard me right) the number of times my husband changed a diaper, my sons took to doody duty almost automatically. They've also been amazingly amiable—considering the hard time I always had getting *them* out of bed in the mornings—when it comes to middle-of-the-night wake-up calls. My daughters-in-law as well have been model moms, showing strength and stability under some extremely stressful circumstances.

I knew things had finally come full circle the night I overheard one of my sons say to his offending offspring, "If I've told you once, I've told you a hundred times." Surely there's nothing more heartwarming than hearing your children repeat something to their children that you said to them if not once—well, a hundred times. It gives you hope. Maybe they really *were* listening.

One thing is for sure: Kids will be kids.

My friend Judy Hopping tells of observing her grandsons Ricardo and Daniel, then ages six and three respectively, as they sat next to each other on the floor watching a DVD movie on television. As big brothers are prone to do, Ricardo was systematically punching Daniel in the arm, only to have little brother, entranced by the movie, ignore him. Not getting the desired response, Ricardo finally quit.

That's when Daniel suddenly reared back and smacked his older sibling right in the face, then quickly turned his attention back to the DVD. Registering surprise and pain, Ricardo burst into tears.

Enter Mom Yvette, who saw only the punch delivered by Daniel. Via a vise grip on his shoulder, Mom stood Daniel up, turned him around, and in a none-too-gentle tone announced that she saw what he did and he was to tell his brother that he was sorry—right now! Daniel refused, Ricardo bellowed, and Yvette firmly restated the instruction.

Finally Daniel walked back over to Ricardo, spread his legs, wrapped his arms around himself, and announced "I am all out of sorrys for him." His mother assured him that he had at least one more sorry in his heart and that she had better hear it now or else.

"Sorry" was quickly spoken, followed by a tearful "That's okay." Then both boys resumed watching their movie.

My guess is at that point Ricardo may have related to the big brother in another grandma story from my friend June Campbell. One morning June was taking two of her grands, Cameron and Kelly, to school. Preschooler Kevin had come along for the ride and was in rare form, not behaving and completely ignoring all attempts at curtailing his antics. That's when Grandma heard Cameron's exasperated voice from the backseat: "I prayed for a brother, and look what I got."

Admittedly, in both cases the grandmas could hardly curtail their comments or chuckles. Somehow, though, they held themselves in check, thanking the Lord not only for healthy, normal grandsons but also ones who had obviously inherited some of their own fathers' childhood behavior.

As I said—payback.

Whatever your outside vocation, being a parent is a full-time position. We already know that. Our children, on the other hand, are just beginning to find out. We can hardly wait for them to ask for help. Problem is, we often don't wait, only to find ourselves once again tangled in the territorial lines.

For instance, while our children are good parents, they have very different parenting styles than we did. In many ways their more laid-back, less up-tight attributes are enviable. They just don't seem to worry as much about appearances or public outbursts. While I've managed to accept the frequent wardrobe malfunctions with a certain amount of grace, it's that last behavioral bit that sometimes has me biting my tongue until it bleeds.

Still, when it comes to offering advice or dealing out discipline, grandparents soon discover they must learn to choose their words and battles carefully. Close as we may be, we are *not* the parents. Even when we disagree with something moms or dads have said or done, we must be careful not to undermine their authority. Except in cases of abuse or neglect, it's important for all concerned that we find some other way or time to express our concern or disagreement. Even then it pays to choose our words and actions wisely. As Proverbs 25:11 poetically proclaims, "Like apples of gold in settings of silver is a word spoken in right circumstances (NASB)." The real reward, if we're careful to earn our children's and grandchildren's love and respect, is that they may then invite us to speak into all their lives.

Every so often, of course, we lose the tongue-biting battle. How well I remember the day I overheard my then 11-year-old grandson, Liam, speak disrespectfully to his mother. Something in me suddenly flared up—maybe a flashback to his father's turbulent teenage years—and I told him in no uncertain terms that I hoped never to hear him speak to his mom that way again. Fortunately for me, his mother seemed to appreciate my interjection rather than be upset.

Even so, I don't know who was more surprised—she, he, or me. Later I made certain to take Liam aside and reassure him that I was not angry with him but rather loved him too much to hear him talk ugly. This also served as a good opportunity to put spiritual legs on the lesson by quoting the middle commandment found in Exodus 20:12: "Honor your father and your mother, so that you may live long in the land the LORD your God is giving you."

That's another good grandparenting ground rule: When it comes to handing down discipline, have a little biblical back-up. Then it doesn't seem so much as though it's just you traipsing past the "No Trespassing" sign.

Speaking of laying down the law, another rule was reestablished the day Liam's younger sister, Olivia, was visiting and decided to defy my repeated solicitations to settle down and stop running around the house. Rather than settling, she streaked sassily up the stairs. Much to her surprise, I bounded after her—yet another benefit of being a grandmother at a still-agile age. I finally cornered her in my walk-in closet, where we had a little heart-to-heart talk among the hangers. From then on there was no doubt that when Gramma speaks, she means business.

This illustrates an important exception as it applies to the delicate matter of who disciplines: When you're at Grandma's house, you play by Grandma's rules.

On the other hand, I believe Grandma's house should represent more than just a place where rules must be rigidly obeyed. In fact, on special occasions it could be just the opposite.

Pat Lorenz tells of the first all-alone visit from her granddaughter, Hailey, who was then four years old and lived 100 miles away. One morning after shopping for shoes, they headed to McDonald's, complete with Playland, for lunch. Afterward, still munching combos and candy, they giggled their way through the funny songs in *Cats Don't Dance*.

Later, as evening and Hailey's appointed bedtime neared, she must have suddenly noticed that there was no attempted enforcement by Grandma. Her next words indicate obvious incredulity that such a perfect day might actually be extended.

"Grammie, are you sure there aren't any rules at your house?"

"I'm sure."

"No bedtime?"

"Nope."

"I can stay up until you go to bed?"

"Yup."

"Until late?"

"Sure. We can sleep late tomorrow. You just snuggle here on my lap, and I'll read you a couple of books."

"I love you, Grammie."

Another grandma wins the award. Yes!

Still, I reiterate, we must know our place, being careful not to overstep our bounds—unless, of course, we can do it in a sweet or sneaky way.

Again Arlene Allen tells of one Christmas when her mother came to visit. Prior to her arrival, Arlene and her son, Rich, had put the finishing touches on the decorations, which included a large Christmas tree in the living room. Their only disagreement came when it was time to turn on the lights. Seems Rich loved for them to blink off and on, a setting that Arlene's sensitivities simply could not abide.

Following dinner that evening, Arlene came around the corner to find her mom and son snuggled together on the living room couch situated directly in front of the tree. Approaching them, she noticed that they both had their eyes tightly closed. Curiosity kept her at a distance. As she watched, they repeatedly opened and closed them. Finally she could stand it no longer.

"What are you two up to?" Arlene asked.

Without missing a wink, her son replied, "We're making the lights blink."

Years later, Arlene discovered with her own grandson something we should all anticipate: sneakiness sometimes backfires. She had decided on one visit that it was time for Grandma to tackle the task of assisting with sex education. For that purpose, she had bought an age-appropriate book that she intended to read to her grandson, one chapter each night.

The first night's lesson went pretty well, her grandson assuring her that, yes, he did understand what they had just read and, no, he really didn't have any questions. Not quite convinced, Arlene decided that the next night they would review the material, just to make sure.

"Is that okay with you?" she asked her grandson, emphasizing that she just wanted to make sure everything was understood.

His reply is priceless. "I got it, Grandma, but if you need to read it again, it's okay with me."

Kind of makes you wonder if the greater grandparenting wisdom might lay in sidestepping the sensitive issues.

Seriously now. Really want to win the best-grandparent award? My advice is easy: Set aside hidden agendas and simply show up. In our quest to be the quintessential grandparents, our *presence* is undoubtedly the best *present* we can give our grandchildren. Trouble is, making time might not always be as easy as it once was.

"One of the most pressing problems grandmothers have these days," reiterates author Pat Lorenz, "is in knowing *how* to be a grandmother. I certainly don't wear cotton flowered dresses or big full-size aprons and bake molasses cookies every week like my Grandma Kobbeman did. I don't sit on a porch swing and rock the evenings away or watch soap operas like my Grandmother Knapp did.

"When I was 50 and a new grandmother, I water-skied behind my brother's boat in Kentucky and snorkeled in the ocean off the coast of two Hawaiian islands. The next year I rode every scary rollercoaster at Disneyland.

"Grandmas are different nowadays. Some have full-time careers, even run corporations and marathons. Others belong to clubs, watch the stock market, eat out a lot, exercise regularly, and still have the energy to do the twist at wedding receptions."

Fact is, with eight grandchildren who all live in other states, Pat laments that she's fortunate if she sees her grandchildren even twice a year. Even then, when they visit she sometimes still finds herself struggling between entertaining them and not neglecting work.

Reflecting on the earlier recorded visit with granddaughter Hailey, Pat states, "Saturday night and Sunday were a breeze, but on Monday morning I began to fret. *I have books to read and review; a proposal to get out. How am I ever going to get it all done if I have to entertain Hailey all day?* Yet with only a day-and-a-half left before Hailey's mother came, I wanted so much to be with her."

That's when the words Pat has laminated on top of her computer got her attention: WRITE THINGS WORTH READING OR DO THINGS WORTH WRITING.

"Suddenly I realized," she states, "that doing things like spending one last day playing with my granddaughter is infinitely more important than sticking to a work routine. Today's grandmother sometimes needs to abandon her schedules and spend a few hours drawing silly animals on the driveway or staring at the leaves from a hammock with a four-year-old's head snuggled in the crook of her arm."

This trail leads us right back to Camp Gramma. After all, isn't camping supposed to be fun and relaxing? Sure, it can be a lot of work. As one not-so-happy-camper friend of mine put it, "Camping is doing what you do at home without all the modern conveniences." For most of us, though, that's the appeal—especially if it's only once or twice a year.

Certainly in the high-tech world our grandchildren are growing up in, the stakes are high. More than ever, children need to be reintroduced to a slower-paced, simpler lifestyle. Sometimes that means not taking the fast lane or the convenient, easy route—like cooking meals over a campfire rather than in a microwave. A few of us middle-age relics remember how to do that. Sure, it takes longer, but wouldn't you agree that more lifelong memories are associated with wood smoke than microwaves? By taking time to share these experiences, we're providing something for our grandchildren that perhaps no one else can.

That's why, even now in our own busy lives, we must be intentional about finding flexibility when it comes to this additional assignment. Still worried about winning? Remember—this doesn't have to be difficult. Again, some of the most important things we do as grandparents don't involve *doing*. They simply involve *being*—another thing I wish I had known when raising my own kids.

Forget about competing. Instead, start creating and cooperating. As our opening psalm reminds us, it's the Lord who assigns us our portion and our cup. He also makes our lot secure. To me, that indicates we each have a job to do and, soliciting His help, needn't be so worried about how we're being rated or where the boundary lines lie.

Here's one final helpful hint. As we're pacing off the grandparenting perimeters of our earthly campsites, remember that the important stakes in all our lives were driven 2,000 years ago on an old rugged cross. As Christians, our most important task is to look for repeated opportunities to make sure our children and grandchildren know that. As Psalm 78:4 states, "We will not hide them from their children; we will tell the next generation the praiseworthy deeds of the Lord, his power, and the wonders he has done." There are some stories only a grandparent can share.

In the end, surely we'll all see and agree that our personal boundary lines have fallen in pleasant places. Let's support each other and celebrate the unique individual impact we can have on this delightful inheritance we've been given. By providing a positive influence, everyone emerges a winner.

CAMP GRAMMA CLIPBOARD #2

Trying to figure out where you fit into your grandchildren's lives? Here are a few simple suggestions to help you be the best grandma or grandpa ever!

- Be yourself. Forget about competing with or copying anyone else.
- Be present. Just being with your grandchildren is often more important than doing things.
- Be careful. Don't overstep your bounds. Use wisdom when offering advice or making comments that might damage your relationship with them or their parents.
- Be creative. Examine your experience, culture, abilities, and interests. What unique skills or insights can you bring to the table?
- Be on the lookout. Watch for opportunities to encourage and expand their interests.
- Be helpful. When possible, offer to baby-sit, chauffeur, help with homework, and so on.
- Be their best encourager and confidante.

3
Sleeping Bags

He will cover you with his feathers, and under his wings you will find refuge; his faithfulness will be your shield and rampart.
—Psalm 91:4

The words I spotted on one cute kid's T-shirt said it all: *I've had it with you people. I'm going to Grandma's!* What do you suppose it is that makes going to a grandparent's home so special? From my own experience, I would say it often provides a soft, safe place in an otherwise harsh and inhospitable world. Symbolically speaking, grandparents serve as sleeping bags on the rocky soil of life.

My Grandma Witt lived in Missouri; I loved going to her house. She was my dad's mother, and though it was a good five-hour drive from our home in Wichita, Kansas, we frequently spent weekends there.

Her three-room house was small but had a big yard boasting things we didn't have in the city: a bountiful garden, a chicken coop, and a well-worn footpath winding down one side. This led to a gate that separated Grandma's property from the lot behind, where a small church sat. Half-way between rested a real curiosity: an old outhouse that, though Grandma had long-ago installed indoor plumbing, anyone desperate enough to brave the spiders could still use. To a child, it was a place alive—literally—with adventure.

Especially during summer visits, I spent more time outside than in—that is, until it started getting dark. Then, no matter what explorations awaited or how many lightning bugs blinked their tiny taillights, I was ready to head inside and hunker down. Grandma's cozy cottage provided the perfect-sized place for a totally tuckered-out kid to cocoon. So secure was it that, once inside, I could sometimes hardly get through dinner before my eyelids started drooping.

That's when, bedrooms being at a premium, Grandma would put down what she called a *pallet,* consisting of several soft quilts piled on the living room couch. No such thing as a sleeping bag in those days, not that Grandma knew of anyway. Sinking into those soft surroundings, lulled by the murmur of adult voices coming from the kitchen and the measured metronome of Grandma's old clock on a nearby shelf, I soon drifted soundly off to sleep.

No doubt, going to a grandparent's place is often fun simply because it's different. Different, however, can't hold a candle to cozy; therein lays the real appeal. My grandmother's house was a place where, even if one awoke during the night, thanks to the old clock's muted gong marking the hours, one always knew the time. During winter visits, the comforting effect was enhanced even more by a small gas stove that softly lit the living room and heated the entire edifice.

By now you've undoubtedly drawn a dubious conclusion. Not only did I grow up in the olden days—I come from hillbilly stock. Yesiree, Bob—and proud of it! My family consisted of simple people who, in turn, made my life seem simple and secure.

I'm sure not everyone reading this has been so fortunate. For some, the memories associated with grandparents are not all good ones. Still, I believe that with a little want-to and will power, any grandparent can be the current catalyst to change, causing new life and beauty to spring from the most knotted family tree.

On top of that, the more tirades I see on television, the more convinced I am that this generation of grandparents must serve not only as a bridge to our grandchildren's past but also as promoters of a positive future. By offering an experienced, optimistic outlook, we can cushion the blows our eternal enemy is throwing through the media, serving as cozy comforters to wrap and buffer them against the cares and craziness of life.

Not that this is anything new.

In her late teens, my friend Jan Coleman faced an identity crisis. The sensational 60s had given way to the psychedelic, sexual revolution of the 70s. This was also the budding age of feminism. As college students, Jan's peers insisted that young women of the day were *not* going to be like their mothers and grandmothers.

"Though I wouldn't admit it to my roommates," says Jan, "I *wanted* to be like my Gramma Hallie—creative, with a sense of peace about her season of life and the choices she had made. Whenever I needed to feel secure about who I was and would become, I popped over to her house across town. She had an uncanny way of making me feel I belonged. As a lonely only child, I relished the time she spent with me, playing Canasta and listening to my endless chatter."

As already mentioned, I, too, was raised like an only child, and that brings me to another appealing feature of going to Grandma's. It was a gathering place. Besides my mom and dad, a steady stream of aunts, uncles, and cousins seemed always to be coming or going while we were there. Some were—how shall I say it?—unusual, even eccentric. Still, it was obvious that they all cared deeply for each other. While there were many interesting exchanges, I don't remember one serious squabble. Rather, the place brimmed with laughter, love, and fond familiarity, memories filling every cupboard and corner.

Not until years later did I realize how much observing this sometimes peculiar pool of people helped form my own opinions and outlook on life. Especially interesting to me is that even my parents acted like different people after arriving—more relaxed and animated. I wonder. Might that have been the real underlying motivation for making the frequent foray?

Speaking of which, ever notice how people will do things when visiting family that they won't do any other time? Possibly it's the fact that we have more free time without the pressure of interruptions or outside commitments. Most likely, though, it's because having history helps our guards come down. No point being pretentious here. We're with people we can trust enough to risk acting like crazy kids again.

That may explain why, when my three now-grown sons come home, much to their own children's chagrin, they inevitably end up in a rollicking wrestling match. And I inevitably end up repairing or cleaning the furniture! Still, I love to see them relaxing and enjoying themselves.

Multigenerational gatherings—good, bad, or completely chaotic—provide everyone present with a sense of purpose, place, and identity. We see not just where we came from, but we recognize to whom we belong. Just like Jan's experience, though the everyday world of school or work may attempt to press us into its mold, going to a beloved grandparent's place grounds us, showing us once again the stuff we're made of.

Grandparents are also the softies who'll spoil a child even at their own expense. This often involves food. One of the things I loved to eat when I was a kid was a big bowl of—don't gag—molasses mixed with butter, and whipped cream right out of the aerosol can, a fairly new novelty in those days. Funny—I don't remember ever eating those two things anywhere other than Grandma's, which probably tells you something. Obviously, in those days none of us worried as much about high fat or cholesterol either; but then, Grandma was skinny as a rail. Oh, that I had inherited those genes!

Good, bad, or indifferent, spoiling is one of the ways grandparents serve to smooth out life's big and little bumps. Sometimes, though, getting spoiled comes with a tiny price tag. Take, for instance, those infamous pet names.

My friend and hairdresser extraordinaire Judy Thompson recently reminisced with a chuckle how her grandfather rarely called her and her siblings by their real names. To him they were Toad, Bear, and Grasshopper, names he had lovingly bestowed upon them.

To this day, my dad was the only one who could get away with calling our youngest son Dusty instead of Dustin. In our house, it's my husband who's dubbed the granddaughters Princess and Pooky, while all the boys are lovingly labeled Bud—a nickname that, not coincidentally, also belonged to Jim's dad. I have my own aliases for each child originating from an ongoing bedtime ritual, something I'll let you in on later.

No doubt there are a few nicknames that need to get lost along the way to adulthood. Still, the mere mention of these monikers inevitably brings back a memory, a smile, or a groan. Silly as they seem, these are names uniquely our own, bequeathed by someone who loves us and sees us as special—an undeniable love language.

This is a point proven by a recent survey. When the question "What does love mean?" was posed to a group of grade-schoolers, here's how one boy identified as Billy, age 4, sweetly summed it up: "When someone loves you, the way they say your name is different. You just know that your name is safe in their mouth."

Well said, William.

My middle son, Derek, reflecting on visits to his own grandparents, shared another comfortingly significant observation: "From the jars upon jars of preserves in the basement waiting for, well, whoever to come to their house that smelled of aged wood and settling earth, there was a simplicity and safety to Grandma's and Grandpa's lives."

Derek seems to have carried something of that simplicity into his own family's experiences. Take camping. Even if they had the money for an RV or cabin, they are no-frills people who would probably prefer a tent. To them, what matters most is having some kind of roof over their heads, food to eat, and their family together having fun.

Despite the constant commercials that urge us to overindulge, isn't that really all most kids require? Yet, like the people who go camping but drag along everything they own, we're all tempted at times to buy in, convinced that for things to be interesting they have to be expensive or complex.

Certainly there are times when having the right equipment helps everyone have a better time. Occasionally it's okay to splurge, as long as we remember that entertaining our children and grandchildren generally doesn't have to be complicated. The most important things are taking time, lavishing love, and allowing them just to be themselves. Whether hanging out in a tent or a high-class hotel, the point is to provide a safe, fun place to be together and do something different.

Thinking back, I would have to say that being at my Grandmother Witt's could have been where the whole concept of Camp Gramma started subconsciously, in the sense that it was a lot like camping out. I just didn't realize it at the time. There were few amenities—indoor plumbing, in fact, being one of the most recent. The old converted gas cook stove still had side compartments where wood had once been stored. There was no dishwasher or microwave oven. If memory serves correctly, a wringer washer sat in an old outdoor shed, and the clothes dryer consisted of two poles in the backyard with wire strung tightly between them. Summer or winter, the clothes were hung out to dry—or freeze. These visits obviously came long before computers and video games, even television! Yet know what's amazing? I never lacked for anything and rarely got bored. Go figure.

Lest you think this a generational glitch, I've noticed the same thing about our grandkids. When the cousins get together, they spend very little time sitting in front of the TV set, preferring instead to play. One exception might be the boys' vacillation toward video games, but at least it's somewhat interactive. Even that has set limits. Like my grandma's linen hanky, I keep a coffer of other interesting alternatives tucked up my sleeve. One of the highlights is that aforementioned old suitcase I stuff with interesting craft and play items collected throughout the year.

Another great thing about setting a less complicated course is that it allows for flexibility. As one memorable-for-all-the-wrong-reasons RV trip to Alaska taught me, a confined space can accommodate only so many people comfortably for so long. Tent stakes, however, can always be stretched. By keeping things simple and unstressed, the campgrounds of our lives can also be enlarged and our borders extended to envelop others. Again, this is important, because there are those who for random reasons have no warm memories of going to Grandma's.

Take my friend Olympia Rossi, for instance. Olympia was born and spent much of her growing-up years in Greece, immigrating with her parents to the United States when she was 11. Though her grandmother spent a few years with them, they never developed a real closeness before her grandmother returned to Greece and passed away.

Olympia's hopes for a better relationship between her children and their grandmother were dashed when her mother died from cancer at an early age. Nor were there any paternal grandparents present since her husband, Max, had also been raised in another country, abandoned by his unwed mother. The paternal grandmother who raised him chose to remain in the home country, making family visits difficult.

Then, through some unexpected circumstances, God serendipitously provided a surrogate. Grandma Nancy, as she came to be called, was a lady they met through an older gentleman in their church. Both had lost their spouses, and she had come to visit in hopes of rekindling an old flame. Though the flame never flickered, she did fall in love—with the Rossi family. For the next eight years this lovely lady made it a point to stay in touch through letters, gifts, and a few return visits, giving Olympia's children a great glimpse into a real grandmother's heart.

By the time Grandma Nancy passed away, a few months before the writing of this book, Olympia's family was grown. As such, some might consider her grandma duty done. Yet does anyone ever outgrow the need for a person who plays such an important role? Olympia informs me that God has now brought Darlene into their lives, another lady willing to widen her boundaries who delights in grandma duty.

Here's another hard thing to grasp. How is it possible to have a plethora of grandparents and still have few feathery-soft experiences? This was a lesson that came home to roost last summer during our fourth official Camp Gramma.

Due to some complicated circumstances resulting from our oldest son's divorce, we are a blended family. We are also a family who long ago made the deliberate decision to show God's love to anyone who comes along through whatever circumstances for however long we can. As a result, his girlfriend, whose own mother passed away a few years ago, and her daughter, Kayla Rose, have become an adopted part of our family.

Kayla Rose is a blonde-haired, blue-eyed cutie who, to our delight, has recently begun calling us Gramma and Grampa. Because Kayla Rose's family history is complicated and convoluted, you can imagine my surprise when one day in the midst of some silly activity she giggled these words: "Gramma, you're the best grandma in the whole world!"

"Thank you, sweetheart," I rather absently replied.

Not sure that I had sufficiently received the message, she restated it: "No, really. I've known a *lot* of grandmas, and you're the best!"

As the impact of her words sank in, my heart was touched. We, with no biological claim on this little kid, have evidently made a mighty impression. May God give us many more opportunities to do so.

The bottom line is this: whether biological or surrogate, there's no place like a truly caring grandparent's home and heart to provide a safe place to settle. The Christmas-card-perfect picture of contentment this brings to mind came during one holiday visit when, entering our family room, I discovered my husband and two small granddaughters snuggled together in an old recliner. All three were sound asleep.

So how can a grandparent guarantee such soft surroundings? First we must settle into our own heavenly Source of comfort. No wonder two of my favorite word pictures are found in Psalm 91. The first two verses state, "He who dwells in the shelter of the Most High will rest in the shadow of the Almighty. I will say of the Lord, 'He is my refuge and my fortress, my God, in whom I trust.'" Then there's verse 4: "He will cover you with his feathers, and under his wings you will find refuge; his faithfulness will be your shield and rampart."

The entire psalm tells of God's love, provision, and protection. Particularly in this present age of uncertainty, these are important spiritual concepts to teach and model for our grandchildren. More enduring than a favorite doll or stuffed toy, trusting and serving God is something every Christian grandparent should pray their children and grandchildren will hold close to their hearts.

Certainly it was my Grandmother Witt's greatest desire for me. That's why every Sunday spent at Grandma's saw us plodding the path past the outhouse to attend services at the little church on the other side of her garden gate. Fact is, our family had donated that piece of their original property so the church could be built there.

Only a few years later, Grandma Witt became too sick to live alone and came to stay with us. During that time we shared a bedroom, which meant I fell asleep every night as Grandma prayed for me.

I was 11 years old when she died. When we went back to Missouri for the funeral, her tiny house was once again packed with people. Consequently, my mom and I spent the night across the street at a neighbor's house, the first time I had ever slept on an old-fashioned feather mattress. Warm though it was, it wasn't like sleeping on Grandma's quilts. And it smelled funny. That's when I first fully realized the hole that losing a grandma leaves in one's heart.

Not long after that, I knelt at the altar in my home church and made a lifetime commitment to serve God. There's no doubt that my grandmother's love and prayers had much to do with that decision. Grandma was gone, but the memories she left would live on.

It was Carl W. Buechner who said, "People may forget what you said, but they will never forget how you made them feel." Not only do grandparents serve as sleeping bags, they also act as memory foam pillows, leaving a lasting impression that our families can always fall back on. I truly believe the more softly we share our faith, the more likely our children and grandchildren will come to understand and accept God's faithfulness.

To illustrate, here's one more memorable story from Arlene Allen: For years she had wanted a memory foam pillow but just couldn't justify the expense. Finally her husband said, "Just do it!" So she did.

Not long after the pricey purchase, her then four-year-old grandson came for a visit. As often happens, he ended up on Grandma's bed watching TV while the adults visited in another room.

It wasn't until time for him to go home that Arlene made a devastating discovery. He had not only pinched off little pieces of her memory foam pillow—he had also stuffed them into the heat vent. The tearful scene that followed probably didn't make a very happy memory, but Arlene does recall taking him aside and assuring him that she wasn't mad at him and still loved him more than any old pillow.

On a recent visit, Arlene asked her now-much-older grandson if he remembered the incident.

"Yes, Grandma," he said, "and I'm still sorry for ruining your pillow."

"I just want you to know," Arlene assured him, "that every time I put my head on that pillow, I think of you."

That, friends, is what memories are made of.

CAMP GRAMMA CLIPBOARD #3

Looking for something soft and sentimental your grandkids will love that doesn't cost a fortune? Here's an idea for a no-sew blanket that even those who are creatively challenged can handle. It's so easy, I make my grands a new one every year. Here's what you do:

- Go to your local fabric store, find the fleece section, then pick out a piece of fleece with a fun pattern. You'll be amazed at all the choices! (Note: I usually look for a print relating to our theme. Monkeys and pirates were easy; spies proved a bit more challenging. I finally ended up with Scooby Doo, the cartoon character who helps his sidekicks solve mysteries. Get it?)
- Once chosen, take the bolt of fabric to the cutting table and have the clerk cut either one-and-a-half or two-yard lengths for each blanket. The first makes an almost 60-inch square; the other is a larger rectangle.
- At home, lay each piece out on your largest surface. Using scissors, trim off the selvage edges (usually these are either white or ragged). If necessary, even up the other sides.
- Starting at any corner, cut fringe all the way around that's approximately three-quarters inch wide and three to four inches deep. Where the cuts intersect at each corner, notch out a square.
- If you want to take time and be fancy, you can knot every two fringes together.
- If you want to be really, *really* fancy, you can lay a same-size piece of solid-color fleece on the back before cutting the fringes, then knot both pieces together as described above. However, this makes the blanket bulkier.
- The single blankets are lightweight, plenty warm, and super-snuggly. Most important, they wash and dry like a dream.

4
Around the Old Campfire

I will open my mouth in parables, I will utter hidden things,
things from of old—what we have heard and known,
what our fathers have told us.
—Psalm 78:2-3

Who can forget the mesmerizing experience of sitting around an evening campfire? Watching as the smoke and sparks drift lazily into the sky, our faces are warmed and transformed—sometimes even spookily distorted—in its flickering play of light and shadow. Each added log sparks a diminutive fireworks display. A heated spec of sap may suddenly explode, shooting a miniscule flaming missile into the shrieking circle of onlookers. As the blaze burns down, we stare reflectively into the flames. What more natural place for songs to be sung, tall tales told, and the deepest secrets shared!

Likewise, bedtime provides the perfect time for grandparents to pass along special stories, songs, and secrets. Whether made-up, real-life, or burning brightly from the Bible, these often become the best-remembered, most-reflected-upon teaching tools.

Of course, anyone who's ever entertained a houseful of grandchildren—or even one, for that matter—knows how hard it can be some nights to get them settled. Following any full day of activity, they're sometimes too rowdy to be ready. Often it's our own fault.

Take our second Camp Gramma, for example. Still basking in the first year's success, I had already decided to follow top TV chef Emeril's advice and "kick this one up a notch." *This year*, I decided, *we'll have a theme.* Poring over a catalog containing party paraphernalia and considering my active, energetic grandchildren, I settled on *Summer of the Monkeys.* Somehow it seemed appropriate.

From crafts to stickers, plates to memo pads, I placed my online order for every imaginable kind of monkey merchandise. When the time came to meet the out-of-towners, I even got the locals to wear monkey-eared head gear to the airport. Should they try to deny having done this, I have photographs.

Activities and outings had again been painstakingly planned—though this year it was make-a-monkey rather than Build-a-Bear—and the treasure chest stuffed with primate paraphernalia. Suffice it to say, we did a lot of monkeying around. No wonder by evening they were all still swinging from the chandeliers.

That's when I discovered the beauty of a bedtime ritual. Like many families, for us this constitutes having one last snack, putting on pajamas, brushing teeth, then curling up with blankets and pillows in front of the old campfire. Actually, in light of our sizzling Sacramento summers, we more often flop around the air-conditioned family room.

Even so, just when I would think they were settled, like that exploding speck of sap, a scuffle or pillow fight might suddenly break out. Then all it took was two magic words: "Story time." Without fail, this resulted in a quick dive under the covers, followed by complete quiet.

No doubt at the end of a long day it's tempting to opt for simply popping in a DVD. But to me, as a writer, book reading is always better. Not only is it hands-on and interactive, it also lets children use their imaginations—something our ever-advancing special-effects technology seems set on squelching. Mind you, I'm not saying movies aren't okay. But really, what theater carries any scent closely comparable to that of ink on new paper or the mustiness of a vintage volume?

Something else that kindled greater interest and excitement pre-TV was the made-up story. Or perhaps some of us have simply failed to fan that flame, either because we're too busy or simply don't see ourselves as story-telling types. If you're one of those, consider this. Experts agree that exercising your brain is good preventive memory-loss medicine. Hmm. Might the early onset of Alzheimer's be avoided or delayed by the mental effort of making up stories? I say it bears consideration.

Seriously, maybe you'll find some motivation in hearing how, as I was pressed into story-telling service during one of our early Thanksgiving visits, my creative efforts to fabricate a fable for my grandchildren established itself as an ongoing tradition. Trying to please both genders and all age groups, I built on three well-established elements: (1) boys like nothing better than superheroes, (2) girls are almost always partial to princesses and, (3) all kids love stories about themselves.

So it was that I made up fictitious fairytale nicknames for the grandchildren, each containing some silly element of individual identification. Fallon became, for obvious reasons, Sir Stinky Socks. Liam, the ever-hungry, is Captain Turkey Drumstick. McKayla, a make-up aficionado, Olivia, with melted-chocolate eyes, and Kayla, middle name Rose, are Princesses Powderpuff, Chocolate Chip, and Rosebud respectively. Though Logan, at age three, is still a bit young to sit through stories, in anticipation we dubbed him Private Pudge.

The ongoing sequels surrounding these colorful characters often incorporate our theme, always involve a villain, and inevitably employ some potentially disastrous or compromising circumstance. Most important, of course, is that our grands' courageous counterparts never fail to come to the rescue and win the day! They *love* these stories, and I love hearing their muffled giggles each time their characters come into play.

Okay. I already hear some reader saying, "That's great for you, but trust me—I'm not that creative!" To borrow a phrase from one of my favorite imaginary *and* imaginative characters, Mary Poppins: "Pish-Posh!"

Just remember—most made-up stories are meant to be silly—usually the sillier the better. Believe me: kids don't care, and on nights when our poor brains are bushed, this relieves a lot of the creative pressure.

Those who are slightly more skeptical might also ask, *How can such silliness possibly have any spiritual impact?*

I see two ways. First, we should make sure whatever story we share somehow helps our grandchildren see themselves and their world in a more positive, productive way. Take a tip from Aesop, and mix in a moral or two. Thus, it becomes a sneaky but entertaining way to slip in self-esteem while weaving moral fiber. Secondly, once you have their attention, it's much easier to move on to something more serious.

For me that means nostalgically pulling out the old Bible Story book that once belonged to their dads. Though at first I picked more familiar stories like Noah's Ark, David and Goliath, or Daniel in the lion's den—those outlining obvious lessons—one night for interest I selected a more obscure tale. Surprise! They liked it just as much. In fact, the more unfamiliar and improbable the storyline, the more they paid attention.

The Bible is, of course, chock full of incredible stories. Soon I found myself digging deep to uncover stuff I had long ago studied, even prompting me to go out and buy a book titled *Amazing and Unexplainable Things in the Bible*.[1] To my surprise, I found myself learning right along with them.

Speaking of which, here's another thing we can learn from our grandchildren: kids' faith has no limits. Nor do they have the hang-ups adults develop when it comes to taking things at face value. All the more reason to make sure we share our stories, biblical and otherwise, while they're still at a young and impressionable age.

Given the daily doses of guff and garbage they get in the world, here's one last helpful hint: Be sure they understand the divine difference between biblical fact and fictional fairy tale.

Such stories are also great tools to stimulate questions and start conversations. To her spiritual credit, my author friend Nancie Carmichael incorporates something into her annual Grandkids' Camp a bit more meaningful than monkeys. She uses a Vacation Bible School model with a theme that focuses on a biblical character. One year, for instance, it was Moses; another year it was Joseph. When telling the stories, she often employs the use of a flannel graph (a board covered in flannel where cut-out pictures depicting the unfolding story are "stuck"), then lets her grandchildren act out the story.

"It's hilarious," states Nancie, "but it helps them 'get it.'" Afterward, her husband, Bill, quizzes them, and they get printed paper dollars called "Bible bucks" for correct answers. These can be redeemed later at Grandma's candy store. Memorizing scripture means even more bucks. "Amazing," concludes Nancie, "how quickly they learn."

Perhaps even more amazing is how much our modern-age kids still enjoy this kind of old-fashioned interaction—not to mention that it works. Even their three-year-old, Hogan, informed his mom one day after returning home that "God made us, and God loves us." If even a toddler can catch that truth, something besides the flannel graph is sticking.

Nancie also agrees that the best time in their Grandkids' Camp is around the evening campfire. They have a fire pit in the backyard where they all sit under the stars and talk. There they share what she calls "high-low"—high meaning the best part of the day, low meaning the worst.

"It's something they all can participate in," says Nancie. "These are the precious, teachable moments when we talk about God and the wonder of His world."

It was after one such poignant, peaceful time of talking to my own grandchildren that I got a particularly unguarded glimpse into Fallon's heart. We had just finished bedtime prayers when he asked if they could turn the TV set on. This is an unfortunate (in my opinion) habit their parents have allowed since they were little to help them fall asleep.

"It's late, buddy—time to go to sleep," I responded. "Let's leave the TV off."

"But we need it to keep from being scared."

"Scared?" Surprise undoubtedly seeped into my voice. "Surely you feel safe at Grandma's house. Besides, you know that God sends angels to watch over us, right?"

"Does it say that somewhere in the Bible?" Fallon's voice quavered.

"It sure does. Let me read it to you." I opened the Bible to Psalm 91, proceeding to share again that personal favorite passage of Scripture describing God's love and care, one that has comforted me through many of my own fearful moments. I particularly wanted him to hear verse 11: "He will command his angels concerning you to guard you in all your ways."

When I had finished, Fallon spoke softly: "I really like it when you read to us from the Bible, Gramma." It was a God-given opportunity to remind them all that the Bible is something they can and should also read for themselves.

Making sure they were settling into sleep, I kissed their sweet cheeks and headed for bed. No sooner had I laid my own sleep-heavy head onto the pillow than something soothing settled on my mind as well. *How many times have I read that portion of Scripture?* I thought. *Yet here it is again, serving as a reminder and reassurance that heaven will be hovering over my earthly ones not only as they sleep but also throughout their lives.* Like those last glowing campfire embers, the ever-applicable wonder of God's Word again warmed my own weary heart.

Discovering Fallon's fear illustrates another important point. Taking time to listen to our grandchildren is equally as important as talking to them. Camp Gramma can provide a safe sounding board, one where secrets and concerns can be shared and kept. As yet another cute t-shirt saying captures it, "What happens at Grandma's stays at Grandma's."

Believe it or not, some of the stories grandkids get the most kick out of—at least when they're little—are the "when I was your age" stories. If these stories sometimes receive an eye-roll, perhaps it's because many miss the all-important reminiscing rule: Resist rambling. Such stories should be interesting but also have a pertinent point.

They might even include a growing-up glimpse of their own parents, though, of course, we must be cautious in what subject matter we choose. Consider, for example, a couple I recently laid on 13-year-old grandson Liam.

Last year Liam entered the new world of middle school. One day I picked him up from school, and almost immediately he launched into a lament about feeling pressure to become part of a certain crowd. Risking that infamous eye-roll, I told him about being a cheerleader in high school and my own struggle in choosing between pleasing my friends—which sometimes meant being pressured to do things or go places I didn't feel right about—and obeying God and my parents. Amazingly, he listened. Or maybe he was just amazed to think that Grandma had actually once been young, popular, and agile.

Then there was the time I caught him smelling his food before taking the first bite. "Just like your Dad," I said with a laugh.

Liam cast a quizzical look. "What do you mean?"

I explained how his dad—our son Derek—had this funny habit as a kid of smelling everything before he ate it. Figuring it was just some quirky phase, we weren't really concerned—until it struck me: *What if he did that at someone else's house? Might they find it rude or offensive?* So I encouraged him to stop, which he did—I thought. Then one day I noticed that now instead, he was touching his food and smelling his *fingers*.

What's so important about these particular parables? These are the stories that speak across generations, providing some inexplicably crazy but comforting sense of connectedness. Due to shortage of experience, children can feel as if they're the only ones who've ever struggled with certain circumstances or fought strange feelings. For youngsters still trying to figure out where in the world they fit in, it can come as a relief to learn from someone they love where their little idiosyncrasies come from. Some unexplained assurance arrives from differentiating between things they may have unavoidably inherited and those merely mimicked. Our selectively shared reflections can help them see that someone has walked that path before, came out okay, and really does understand.

Here's a cute case in point from author Tonya Ruiz. One day Tonya and her daughter and two grandchildren stood huddled together in a tiny bathroom staring down the commode. Clogging it was the fuzzy pink blanket belonging to Tonya's 17-month-old granddaughter.

Don't you think it's funny, Grandma? her granddaughter's dancing eyes seemed to say, looking up at her as an ally. Firstborn brother—who would never have pulled such a shenanigan—stood nearby like a solemn soldier.

Tonya admits wanting desperately to laugh at the spunky toddler's antics, but seeing her daughter's distress, she didn't want to get either one of them in trouble. So she stifled it, watching instead as Mom pulled the soggy blanket from the toilet bowl and placed it into a bucket for its journey to the washing machine.

The next day when her granddaughter tossed the TV remote into the toilet, Tonya's mirth became impossible to contain. Why? Seems as a child Tonya herself had a flushing fascination, once likewise attempting to drown her jack-in-the-box. It's a story she'll undoubtedly share with her granddaughter when she gets older.

If there's anything I've learned from short-lived forays into various retail ventures, it's that you can sell almost anything if it comes in the right wrapping. In the same way, our wrapped-in-love stories may help "sell" our grandchildren on a spiritual concept or two.

Maybe that's why our son Derek mostly remembers his grandpa's rye wit and the quick joke he seemingly kept stored in his back pocket, just waiting for the right moment to pull it out. "The man had an incredibly easy way about him," Derek reflected recently, "and genuinely seemed to enjoy life."

Thinking of my dad reminds me of yet another way grandparents pass on their love, laughter, and lessons: through music. Aside from his crazy quips, Dad was frequently heard whistling or humming some familiar old hymn, not to mention his repertoire of silly songs. One called "Perky Doodle Di Doe"—yet another infamous hillbilly high jink—accompanied by a jolly jig never failed to send our kids into gales of giggles.

Then there are the quaint, sentimental songs grandparents sing. Judy Thompson tells of one her mother taught her grandson, Travis. Listen to the love lesson in these lyrics:

> *Put me in your pocket, where I'll be close to you.*
> *No more will I be lonely, no more will I be blue;*
> *And when we two must part, dear,*
> *There'll be no sad adieu,*
> *For I'll be in your pocket*
> *And I'll go along with you.*

How could any kid feel frightened about being alone after hearing that tune a few times? Or how about the popular song my mother sang titled "I Love You a Bushel and a Peck," first recorded by Doris Day in the 1950s.

These are the types of catchy tunes telling how much we're loved and thought of. Years later, all we have to hear is the melody for an image of the person who sang it or the place we first heard it to appear magically—not to mention the flood of warm, fuzzy feelings.

How about songs designed to teach a lesson or instill a principle, perhaps even plant some simple theological seed? A lot of us learned these in Sunday School. Friend and ministry colleague Sam Huddleston tells how one such song literally saved his life.

Speaking to a group of ministers, Sam related how when he was eight years old his Sunday School teacher, Mrs. Harding, a grandmother many times over, taught her class a simple song titled "Jesus Wants Me for a Sunbeam."

A sunbeam, a sunbeam, went the chorus, *Jesus wants me for a sunbeam. A sunbeam, a sunbeam*, it repeated, *I'll be a sunbeam for Him.* Along with that, she would tell them every week how Jesus loved them, had a plan for their lives, and wanted them to shine brightly for Him.

"I grew up and became everything *except* a sunbeam for Jesus," Sam said.

Sadly, when he was still in high school, Sam and a cousin made the disastrous decision to rob a convenience store. In one sudden, irrational act, Sam's cousin stabbed the store clerk, who later died. That's how, at 17, Sam found himself sentenced to life in prison as an accomplice to murder.

Then one day, while he was cleaning up his cell, the words to that childish song inexplicably started going through his mind. "Only this time," Sam recalls, "the words I heard were *Jesus* still *wants you for a sunbeam; will you be a sunbeam for him?*" So real and profound was that experience, Sam claims he looked around his cell for Mrs. Harding.

While still in prison Sam re-surrendered his life to Christ and started finally to live out the words to that song. Not coincidentally, five years into his life sentence he was miraculously released—

an amazing story that he's penned in his book *Five Years to Life*.[2] That's when he started a new life sentence—preparing for full-time Christian ministry.

Years later, while on a missions trip in Africa, Sam got a call from his mother saying Mrs. Harding was very ill and that he should call her. He did so right away.

"Where are you calling from, and what are you doing?" the surprised Mrs. Harding asked Sam.

"I'm in Africa," Sam responded, "trying to make sunbeams for Jesus."

Across the phone lines came her chuckle. "You'll never forget that song, will you?"

Sam's smiling answer was "I can't."

There's no doubt that putting words to music helps us remember. Think, for instance, about those catchy TV commercial tunes that keep products prancing through our heads. How much more important it is to make sure spiritual truths stay with our grandchildren all their lives! Sing 'em out, sidekicks—even if, as my dad would say, we can't carry a tune in a bucket.

Some of the songs we teach our grandchildren may even come back to bless us in ways and at times we could never imagine. Consider one especially touching story I recently read on a blog once belonging to fellow author Kristy Dykes.

At the time, Kristy and husband, Milton, were also comrades in ministry, pastoring a wonderfully caring church in Florida. Imagine the shock and sadness their congregation, family, and friends felt when Kristy announced that she had been diagnosed with a terminal brain tumor.

As those who loved her prayed fervently, Milton faithfully shared her post-surgery progress online, often reflecting on their family journey as well. That's where I found the following story.

Seems their three-year-old granddaughter, Claudia, was walking with Milton down a resort hotel hallway last summer.

With great animation and talking hands, she said, "Papa, Jesus is strong. Jesus is verrry stronggg."

"I know," Milton responded.

Meaning to make her point, she repeated, "But Papa, Jesus is very, very strong!"

Suddenly her insightful words sank in, and Milton couldn't contain his curiosity as to the toddler's source of such theology.

"How do you know Jesus is strong?" he asked.

Claudia sang her answer:

> Jesus loves me! this I know,
> For the Bible tell me so.
> Little to ones to Him belong;
> They are weak, but [with great gusto] He is strong.

Milton melted over her childlike faith and enthusiasm. How could he have possibly known then how soon the words from this simple Sunday School song would return, providing a source of hope and strength in the face of Kristy's uncertain future? Only a few months later she passed away.

"Surely we've had our times of weakness," Milton admits, "but through it all the Lord has remained strong for us."

There are songs and stories that only a grandparent can share. How much family history, how many lifelong lessons may be lost if we don't? Above the many voices vying for our grandchildren's attention, let's make sure ours is heard. As Moses admonished the children of Israel in Deuteronomy 4:9, "Only be careful, and watch yourselves closely so that you do not forget the things your eyes have seen or let them slip from your heart as long as you live. Teach them to your children and to their children after them."

Tonya Ruiz sums it up: "There are many things that we can pass along to our children and grandchildren—stories of times gone by, of events in our lives, and of people who are no longer with us—but we should also make sure that we take time to read them the Bible. Through its rich history, happenings, and characters, we teach them of God's grace, guidance, and forgiveness."

So how about it? Start stockpiling your own selection of Bible-inspired books, stories, and songs. Then, when the opportunity arises, you'll have plenty of fuel for the old campfire.

CAMP GRAMMA CLIPBOARD #4

Surely those who are lifelong book-lovers understand the desire to leave stories as a legacy for their grandchildren. Statistics still show that (1) children who are read to will likely become readers, and (2) lessons taught in the form of stories are remembered longer. The hard part—if you don't already have family favorites—may be deciding what to read. Here are some general book-shopping guidelines:

- Every family should own a good basic Bible storybook. Check out the selection at your local Christian supply store, or go to <www.christianbook.com>. There you'll find a ton of great new titles as well.
- As for secular selections, the safest thing is sticking to the classics. Books like *The Velveteen Rabbit, Charlotte's Web,* and *The Chronicles of Narnia* contain positive moral messages that speak to all ages, undoubtedly accounting for their popularity and longevity.
- While secular book stores also have wonderful children's sections, here's one word of caution. Be sure to thoroughly research any popularly advertised titles, as some may contain subversive underlying messages masked in a story that seems otherwise innocent. One recent example is *The Golden Compass,* the first book in a trilogy trying to mimic the C. S. Lewis Narnia classics but written by an author with an atheist agenda.
- Don't want to spend a fortune? Check out thrift stores, or visit the library.
- Don't discount occasional DVDs, but make them interactive by choosing those with moral or spiritual messages that can be discussed afterward.

Give made-up stories a shot!

- Start with something short and silly. Kids don't care!
- Share a funny family tale or two, maybe even one involv-

ing the grandkids. Just make sure it's positive. No poking fun allowed.
- Some family stories bear not only repeating but also recording for posterity.

As for songs—
- Pass along the ones you learned as a child—silly, sentimental, and from Sunday School. Kids especially enjoy those that involve hand motions and dance steps.
- Don't have a musical heritage? Check Christian bookstores for children's music CDs. Older kids might enjoy learning the songs from an age-appropriate children's musical. One of the VBS programs I chose had an accompanying CD of songs.
- Whatever you choose, remember: Songs that are simple and repetitive are the easiest to learn.

5
May I Have S'mores, Please?

> *He provides you with plenty of food and*
> *fills your hearts with joy.*
> —Acts 14:17

"Da problem in dis country is dat eff'ryone is busy vorking! Kids here haf no one around to keep dem out uf trouble."

The shopkeeper's eastern European accent carried across the counter of the quaint antique store I had serendipitously discovered while waiting for my husband to finish a meeting near San Francisco. Looking for a frugal "find," I got more than I had bargained for. One innocent inquiry about his origins opened a floodgate of impassioned opinion, particularly about young people with too much time and not enough nurturing.

"In my country," he continued, "ve tink tree tings only are important: kinder, kirche, and kuchen—children, church, and kitchen."

When it comes to keeping out of trouble, I could certainly connect the first two. The word *kitchen*, however, captured my attention. Why didn't he simply say "home"?

Then, like the smell of soup simmering on a cold winter day, it hit me. Of all the memories associated with home and family, don't the warmest call to us from the kitchen, conjuring up visions of times spent together around the table? Leaving the shop, I carried the proprietor's interesting alliteration—and an antique German cookie jar—along with me.

I've already mentioned getting to eat gooey things at my grandmother's that I didn't get at home, but there was sustaining stuff too. Seems, in fact, that Grandma was always in the kitchen cooking up something good. As also previously recorded, I come from a long line of farmers and foragers. Being one-quarter Cherokee Indian, Grandma Witt often searched the surrounding woods for wild greens and berries. This, along with whatever the men folk hauled in from hunting, resulted in some delicious if unusual meals. Still, whether we were savoring squirrel or squash, being together was what made the meal memorable.

Nowadays, of course, most of us do our foraging at the local food market and are more likely to make things in the microwave than stir them up from scratch, but the principle is the same. Times around the table bring families together.

Allow me one quick side step onto the old soapbox. If there's one postmodern principle I would like to nuke, it's the way some parents allow their children to graze through the kitchen rather than taking time to sit down and eat properly. Sure, they get the nutrition needed for their bodies, but their souls miss something special. As for my own grands, whatever they do at home, grazing at Gramma's is, as the shopkeeper would say, verboten!

'Nuf said.

Though I still personally prefer made-from-scratch meals, I admit that the advantage of convenience foods is that they save time otherwise spent slaving over the stove. This leaves more minutes for making merry. Even so, sans modern conveniences, my grandma somehow still made time for fun. Often she would incorporate it right into the meal, doing something silly like unexpectedly pushing out her top denture. Sometimes it just slipped; either way, it was hilarious. The message that also slipped out was this: food, fun, and family can be successfully served up together.

Another thing we groovin' grannies get to do more now days is eat out. For my last birthday, to keep me from cooking, my family took me to a local restaurant. It was a thoughtful, though expensive, gesture and great fun to have everyone together.

"Anyone want dessert?" Jim asked at the end of the meal.

Everyone was full, so I suggested we go back to our house for coffee and whatever was on hand.

"Do you have dessert at home?" he asked.

"Not really," I admitted.

That's when seven-year-old Olivia piped up excitedly. "I know, Gramma. We could make birthday cookies!"

My heart was touched. Cookie-making had been our special thing to do since she and her cousins were old enough to stand on a chair and stir. Now, to Olivia, any special occasion meant cookies or cupcakes.

"Then," she added, "we can eat 'em!"

Landing laughs all around, this also stirred up another important ingredient: the joy of making things often rivals or surpasses the joy of eating them. Either way, the key word is *joy*. Between the fancy restaurant dinner and making cookies, which do you suppose my granddaughter will remember longer?

Truth is, if it had been anyone else's birthday, we would have been home eating my famous traditional Braddy birthday lasagna. Every time I make it, a message seems to magically bubble to the surface: "You're special. Look what I made just for you!"

Certainly no memory associated with a grandparent's place is stronger that the smell of something wonderful cooking or baking. Food is yet another language of love. As that plump perpetrator in the Pillsbury commercials reminds us, "Nothin' says lovin' like somethin' from the oven"—or in some cases, the frying pan and griddle.

One of Derek's most vivid vacation memories is that of waking up to discover his grandpa standing over an iron skillet full of sizzling bacon. For his brother Damon, it was Grandpa's pancakes. What warms my griddle, though, is how they both remember his merry whistle. To my dad, an established early riser, making breakfast was a labor of love. Whistling served as his constant culinary companion.

Interesting, isn't it, how so many foods are reminiscent not only of special events but of people—even, or especially, when we can't understand the appeal. Dustin still grimaces when he remembers how Grandpa loved cornbread crumbled up in buttermilk. Yuck!

Not so yucky, though, was the kitchen drawer he kept full of candy bars. A confirmed candy-holic, my dad would watch for them to go on sale, then buy a ton at a time. To the delight of my own grands, it's a tradition I carry on. No visit to Gramma's is complete without a hug, a kiss, and a dash to the candy cupboard—not necessarily in that order.

Here's what it boils down to. Food not only sustains our stomachs—it also lifts our spirits. Judy Thompson tells how her mom left an established career to baby-sit Judy's then-toddler son. Travis was her last grandchild; no way was she going to miss that opportunity. The big bonus was that when Judy dropped him off in the morning, her mom would not only have breakfast waiting for both of them but also a lunch packed for her to take to work as well.

"As if that wasn't enough," remembers Judy, "she'd often send us home in the evening with 'extra' dinner."

What Grandma couldn't know was how her culinary contributions were nurturing not just their bodies but also their souls. During this time Judy was dealing with some sad circumstances associated with her difficult, deteriorating marriage, a matter she had chosen not to concern her parents with until she finally decided to flee. No question—Travis was having a tough time too. Thus, Grandma's house wasn't just a restaurant but also a refuge.

"I don't know what we would have done during that time without my parents' love and support," Judy tells me today, then laughs as she adds, "and food!"

Quite simply, but not insignificantly, food comforts, communicates, and keeps people connected. This is something with which one of my all-time favorite authors, Jan Karon, concurs. In writing, she attributes the popularity of her six-book series surrounding the tiny, fictional town of Mitford partially to the fact that good home cookin' is braided into the books' fabric like a rag rug—so much that it eventually prompted her to compile a cookbook based on the characters' recipes and stories.[1]

"Food is something we all understand," Karon writes. "It's a common language. And it's one more way readers are encouraged to feel at home in Mitford."

No doubt, a good meal makes even strangers feel welcome. It also provides a forum around and about which to talk. "This is delicious!" "Would you share this recipe?" "How 'bout another helping?" "So how's the family?" What more relaxed place is there to share faith and feelings than sitting around the kitchen table with a full tummy? The most important ingredient, of course, is to begin by asking God's blessing—another important but sometimes overlooked ingredient. Then, like the table, the spiritual tone, too, will be beautifully set.

Interestingly, Ms. Karon also attributes the profusion of food in her books to the fact that initially she was writing hungry. She had left a successful career in advertising to write full time, something that didn't immediately pay off. For the first year, her cupboards were largely bare. So what do you do when you don't have food? You imagine it.

That's not a bad thing, especially when, as in the case of the prodigal son, food is so closely associated with family that it turns your thoughts toward home. Reading Luke 15:17-18, we can almost hear the transgressor's tummy grumbling. "When he came to his senses, he said, 'How many of my father's hired men have food to spare, and here I am starving to death! I will set out and go back to my father and say to him: Father, I have sinned against heaven and against you.'" To me this illustrates how memories connected to food and family can create not only physical but spiritual hunger.

The importance of building family memories and traditions, especially as it relates to our wandering ones, is something I elaborate on in my book *Prodigal in the Parsonage*. Consider the following words from the chapter titled "Home Is Where the Hurt Is"[2]:

> These [traditions, memories] are things that hopefully they'll miss enough somewhere down the prodigal path to be drawn back. I have to believe the biblical prodigal sitting in that pigpen must have mentally maneuvered every familiar room in his father's house more than once. And dreamed at night about sleeping in his own bed. We know for certain that he thought about food. Every family has their favorite special meals. If there's anything that will bring our boys running from the distant land, it's biscuits and gravy for breakfast or the traditional Braddy birthday lasagna.

Surely there is something special about the companionship of sharing a meal. We not only miss the food—we also miss the fellowship of those around the table, a sensation strong enough to draw us back to a place of safety and security.

Undoubtedly that's why, when my mother got sick and had to be placed in a nursing home, my dad lost his appetite. It wasn't until I came to visit that he decided, though his heart still ached, he might feel better if he ate something. Certainly he missed Mom's great cooking. We all did! But mostly he missed having someone there to share the meal. Even great food doesn't taste that great when you're eating alone.

It's heartwarming to hear that this is a lesson not lost on the young. Vivian and David Ross are pastor friends of ours who have 26 grandchildren and 9 great-grands. Shortly before Christmas one year, Vivian and David were keeping seven-year-old Alex while his parents attended a meeting.

"What do you want for Christmas, Alex?" asked Grandpa. To their surprise, Alex responded that he didn't need any toys—he just wanted a big feast. His exact words were "Just everybody being together and having a good meal with stuffing."

Not sure exactly what he meant by stuffing, Grandma asked him to explain.

"You know, the kind that goes inside."

Though Alex was obviously referring to what was tucked in the turkey, somehow his short experience had showed him that what's inside people is also more important than the outward trappings. No question. Grandma and Grandpa were proud to see him relish the real meaning of Christmas.

One of the favorite food-related Christmas traditions Jan Coleman has established with her grandchildren is decorating a gingerbread house.

"I buy extra candies and gum drops because we eat as many as we put on the house," Jan says with a laugh, then a lament. "It's quite a creative endeavor, even though it's demolished a day later." The memories they build, though, can never be destroyed.

Speaking of Christmas automatically turns our thoughts toward things traditional, table-top and otherwise. Join me in a short jaunt down a side trail to explore the latter.

"Family traditions," states friend and author Peggy Musgrove in a recent online article, "play a significant part in our celebrations and tie our families together. Using Grandma's china, making the customary family recipes, and hanging the hand-knitted stocking by the fireplace are typical of traditions that mold family members into a unit."

When her girls were elementary school age, on the sides of tall tapers they marked the number of days until Christmas. Each day they read Christmas stories while the candles burned the allotted amount for that day.

"That way," says Peggy, "we knew exactly which day we were going to Grandma's!"

Even non-food traditions often take place around the table. In the case of my friend, Mary Ann Cole, that's where she spreads out all the photos and materials that go into making scrapbooks chronicling her grandchildren's lives. These become gifts each grandchild receives, without disappointment, upon high school graduation.

Disappointment did come, though, the year Mary Ann decided to break another longstanding family tradition. Every Christmas since her grands were born she's given everyone, including moms and dads, new pajamas. One Christmas, assuming they were getting too old, she decided to pass on the pj's.

"You wouldn't believe the uproar," claims Mary Ann, "when the last package was opened and no pajamas appeared!" Needless to say, they've since made an annual encore appearance.

With the Braddy bunch, it's boxer shorts and "snugglies"—the latter being something I picked up from friend and surrogate grandma Nita Sweet during our days of living in Alaska. Those who've read my book *True North* know that, being far from family, Alaska's a place where tradition takes on increased importance. That's why every Christmas, no matter how old Nita's two boys got, she always made sure they got what she called a "snuggly" in their Christmas stocking—usually some kind of stuffed animal. Though now we're all scattered across what Alaskans call the "lower 48," and both her boys are long-married with children of their own, my guess is that Grandma Nita is still sending those seasonal snugglies.

There are times when, to reveal the real significance, traditions need to be tweaked. As with many families, it has been our practice to read the biblical Christmas story every year before plunging into our presents. This year, a comment from Olivia caused me to give that tradition a different twist.

Riding in the car one day, I listened as she chattered on about Santa and other seasonal stuff.

"That's all fun," I replied, "but you know the real reason for the holiday, right? It's Jesus' birthday."

"I didn't know that," she said.

Didn't know? My mind reeled. *How could she not know when we talk about it every year?* Then I realized that since her family hasn't attended church regularly, nor are public schools any longer allowed to make specific religious references—though children are bombarded earlier every year with the secular symbols of the season (grrr!) like snowflakes in California—the real meaning of Christmas was simply not sticking.

Since I hadn't yet put out my nativity sets, the next day I had Olivia and Liam help me, adding each character as Grandpa read that part of the Christmas story. My hope is that attaching action to the words will help make a more lasting impression.

Point in fact, especially when it comes to traditions that carry spiritual significance, we can't assume that our grandchildren automatically get it. As Peggy says about the candle-burning countdown she and her girls practiced each Christmas, "It was a beautiful tradition, but, like other family traditions, it was only a pretty wrapping, not the gift." As keepers of both the hearth and our grandchildren's heritage, it's our task to make sure they understand the underlying importance of these repeated practices.

It's easy in the chaos of large family gatherings for meaning to get lost. Weary in well-doing, we can even begin to wonder whether it's worth all the effort. That's why Galatians 6:9-10 admonishes us, "Let us not become weary in doing good, for at the proper time we will reap a harvest if we do not give up. Therefore, as we have opportunity, let us do good to all people, especially to those who belong to the family of believers." The key, of course, is not making ourselves too weary to haul in the harvest.

In light of that, maybe what's needed is some new inspiration. Consider the following fun-feasts cooked up by some of my Camp Gramma colleagues.

Connie Clements lives in Oregon and does what she calls a Cousins' Camp each year. Smarter than some of us, she sets stricter limits. Hers lasts only a few days and allows only those at least four years old and potty-trained to attend. During those days, they rent or borrow a large-enough vehicle to transport everyone to a cabin.

"It's chaotic," Connie admits, "but memorable!"

The real reason they do it, though, is relaxingly rational. Once there, they take hikes, swim for hours, and occasionally trek into town to spend "dollars" earned by performing camp chores. Evenings are often spent simply watching family-friendly movies.

Despite the chaos, Connie still manages to set a spiritual tone. "Last year's camp landed on a Sunday," she writes, "and we had our own church service. It was a beautiful morning, so we sat out on the deck. The kids chose the worship choruses and shared some personal testimonies and prayer requests. Then my husband gave a short spiritual message."

Another now three-year tradition they started was having a birthday party for Jesus complete with party hats, gift bags, balloons, and even a yard sign that says HAPPY BIRTHDAY, JESUS. Even though it's summer, Connie reads a different Christmas storybook every year, once adding an award-winning companion video.

"We have an easy lunch like hotdogs or pizza," Connie says, "and I always have a group craft."

One year they all made a gingerbread house together. Another time Connie found felt neck scarves at the dollar store and let each one decorate one with glittery glue and stickers.

"It was great," she reflects, "watching the older ones helping the young ones. We always end the party by singing 'Happy Birthday' to Jesus."

Seems they've truly caught the celebrate-Christmas-all-year-long concept.

One funny story surfaced when the campers headed into town looking for ways to spend their camp bucks. Then-five-year-old Elijah proudly told the lady at the five-and-dime checkout counter, "We're all cousins! We're with our grandma and papa at Cousins' Camp." What made it funny? This was pretty obvious since everyone was wearing the custom, logo imprinted t-shirts Connie orders every year boasting ANNUAL CLEMENTS COUSINS' CAMP.

With eight energetic campers to corral, Ann Gibson's Cousins' Camp runs on a little tighter budget. Rather than taking everyone to a cabin or some costly theme park, the grandkids camp at her house. With a two-adults-to-eight-kids ratio, this keeps both kids and expenses safely surrounded. They then make field trips to interesting areas and local historical spots.

"Now that we all live in California," says Ann, "we've been a huge part of several grandkids' fourth-grade state history projects."

Some constants in her camp plans also include t-shirts along with bags containing a plethora of practical things—lip balm, toothbrush and toothpaste, and flashlight. Ann also uses this as a time to teach about responsibilities such as helping with meals and camp cleanup, how to treat each other, and keeping your "face and space" clean. Guidelines are given for use of technology too.

"IPods are allowed," states Ann, "but no DSs, TV sets, or laptops."

Aside from the usual camp activities, here are some events Ann recalls were great hits. Though a lot of the prep and planning fell on her, one year all the kids tie-dyed their camp shirts. Another year's winner was Grandpa's yo-yo collection and demonstration, as was taking the ferry to San Francisco and spending the day wandering around the wharf and other sights.

Their final day together requires a plan involving all the parents who happen to be around. One year the kids prepared and served them a formal dinner. This meant getting all dressed up and learning how to serve properly, speak politely, and so on. They even created a big finger-painted banner.

Obviously Ann is trying to instill in her grandchildren the importance of respecting each other, which includes politeness, neatness, and service. Perhaps the best opportunity provided to demonstrate these still-fledgling skills are visits to Grandma Great, their name for Ann's mother.

Crafts, too, can quickly bring everyone circling around the table. For that inspiration, Nancy Carmichael relies on trips to the local craft store. In the same spirit of service, this sometimes involves making gifts to give their parents.

"This last summer," says Nancy, "we painted clay pots and planted herb gardens in them. The summer before, my husband helped them make birdhouses. They loved it and have kept them as souvenirs."

Bringing us back to the food-related traditions, Nancy's grands do an annual lemonade stand, then take the earnings into town and spend them. Their excursions include trips to the lake and local fish hatchery, plus her husband, Bill, takes the older ones on bike rides to the general store.

At this point someone is surely saying, "Why on earth would any un-addled grandparent grapple with all these things?" The answer is easy: for heaven's sake.

Seen from an eternal perspective, there is so much more to our motives than just fun and games. Nancy puts it this way: "I think it's pretty much a baby-boomer thing to do grandkid camps." Most grandparents today *are* of that generation. "But these are also powerful vehicles to provide opportunities for instilling God's truth in our precious ones."

These are times, too, for teaching and modeling the joy of serving others. I'm sure you noticed how a number of the mentioned activities revolve around just that. Somehow we must help our grandchildren see how all this trivia translates into something deeper and more enduring: serving God and loving each other. That's why dishing up a good attitude and sweet spirit is also of primary importance.

Truth is, some things can't be taught—they must be caught. To quote something I saw painted on a ceramic plate, "If God had meant us to use recipes, He wouldn't have given us grandmothers."

Let's be honest: there's no predicting how things will go when a large group gets together. The best plan is to have an alternate plan—or give up the plan altogether. Whatever happens, don't let disappointment dampen your spirits. The bright side is that some of the best and most lasting memories are the result of plans that went kaput!

Perhaps the reason some start seeing this as a chore is because they expect every event to be picture-card perfect. Yet anyone who's ever made s'mores—that delectable concoction combining graham crackers, chocolate bars, and melted marshmallows—knows that inevitably someone will drop his or her in the dirt gooey side down. Or somebody's marshmallow will melt off the stick and fall into the fire.

Another potential party-pooper is that there will inevitably be times after expending much effort when we'll feel unappreciated. If you're like me, you may spend hours preparing something that takes your family 10 minutes to devour.

That's when it pays to keep Colossians 3:23-24 on your back burner: "Whatever you do," Paul tells these the Colossian campers, "work at it with all your heart." Now here's the clincher: "as working for the Lord, not for men, since you know that you will receive an inheritance from the Lord as a reward. It is the Lord Christ you are serving."

Again, the real reason we do all these things must remain the menu's main entrée. Not only do we want that inheritance as a reward for ourselves—we want our children and grandchildren to receive it too. My advice? Do your best, and let God do the rest.

Here's where the flapjack hits the griddle. As the older generation, grandparents are most often the ones responsible for passing on recipes, establishing traditions, providing unexpected opportunities, and teaching important truths, spiritual and otherwise. The sobering fact is that this is our last best shot at hands-on family influence. Our greatest hope is that the next generation will pick up principles from us that they'll find important enough to emulate, then pass them on. Like anything we prepare for our families, our greatest joy comes when hearing someone say, "May I have s'more, please?"

As for the antique shopkeeper's statement about kids in this country having no one around to keep them out of trouble, I must take exception.

We're called grandparents.

CAMP GRAMMA CLIPBOARD #5

Looking for an easy way to start your grandkids' collection of favorite family recipes? Simply copy them onto 3 x 5 cards, then slip into the plastic sleeves of an inexpensive 4 x 6 size photo album. Voilà! Kid-sized cookbooks that are easy to keep clean.

Here are a couple of camp-time favorites to start with:

S'MORES

Ingredients
Plain or cinnamon graham crackers
Large marshmallows
Plain Hershey's chocolate bars

Directions: Break graham crackers in half, and place a same-size square of chocolate on top. Set aside. Carefully push marshmallows onto a long-handled stick or metal fork, and hold over campfire, fireplace, or stove burner until outside is toasted and middles are melted. Squish hot marshmallow onto the waiting chocolate-graham and sandwich with another cracker square. Enjoy!

GRAMMA'S SUGAR COOKIES

Ingredients

2/3 c. shortening	4 tsp. milk
3/4 c. sugar	2 c. flour
1/2 tsp. grated orange peel	
1-1/2 tsp. baking powder	
1 egg	
1/4 tsp. salt.	
1/2 tsp. vanilla	

Directions: Thoroughly cream shortening, sugar, orange peel, and vanilla. Add egg; beat till light and fluffy. Stir in milk. Sift together dry ingredients; blend in creamed mixture. On lightly floured surface, roll dough to 1/8-inch thickness. Cut in desired shapes with cookie cutters. Bake on greased cookie sheet at 375 degrees for about 6-8 minutes or until edges are golden. Cool slightly; remove from pan. Cool on rack. Decorate. Makes 2 dozen.

EASY FROSTING

Melt 3-4 T. butter. Keep mixing in powdered sugar and a few drops of condensed milk until frosting reaches spreading consistency. Add food coloring as desired and use right away or cover. If using sprinkles, they should be added before frosting hardens.

If you're looking to adopt a tradition or two, here are some classics shared by others that you might consider.

- Like Jan and her grands, try tackling a gingerbread house. Admittedly Jan takes the easy route by purchasing a pre-baked kit but buys extra frosting and candy trimmings. Everything is constructed on a stiff cardboard base covered with foil. Once it's finished, Jan helps the kids cut out and decorate Christmas figures—trees, Santas, sleds, and so on—and place them around the base. The decorations come from Grandma Jan's handy-dandy box of year-round craft items.
- Martha Bolton's Christmas decorating tradition begins even before Thanksgiving is over. On Thanksgiving evening, after the family's eaten first, seconds, and in some cases thirds, Martha starts pulling out the Christmas decorations so the kids can help her decorate.

"It's so much fun to watch the kids setting up the Christmas village, hanging the garland, and arranging all the rest of the decorations," says Martha. "I especially enjoy doing this because my house gets decorated early, and it pulls the whole family into the festivities."

According to Martha, even the men folk enjoy seeing the familiar decorations coming out of the boxes. Hmm. Kinda makes you wonder if she's related to that *other* media Martha, doesn't it?

- She also allows the grandchildren to set up the Nativity set, letting them play with it and get familiar with the story of Jesus' birth. No "hands off" policy here.

    One year her youngest granddaughter set it up in a little different way. "Her family was about to be blessed with twin brothers," says Martha, "so she took another manger from one of my many smaller Nativity sets and placed it in the main one. In her mind, babies came in twos, even babies born in mangers!"

    Martha took a picture, then turned it into an occasion to talk about how much the one and only baby Jesus means to the world—something we can all be thankful for on Thanksgiving or any other day.

6
Blazing a Trail

*Blessed are those whose strength is in you,
who have set their hearts on pilgrimage.*
—Psalm 84:5

"Everyone has to die sometime."

I entered the room just in time to overhear my darling but direct-to-the point daughter-in-law attempting to prepare her children for the fact that Grandma and Grandpa might not always be around.

"Remember," Deirdra continued—"Grandma and Grandpa are much older than us."

Thanks a bunch.

Liam's gorgeous gray eyes widened with incredulity. *Uh-oh*, I thought. *He's not taking this well.* As he turned those befuddled blinkers on me, I prepared to counter his concerns about our ongoing existence.

"But if you guys die," he queried, "who's going to pay for everything?"

Huh?

Good question. Aren't grandparents, after all, the ones who are most often in a position to financially provide their grandchildren with special outings and opportunities? Not that we're all rich. It's just that by this stage of the game we've likely managed to accumulate most of the material things we need. Hopefully in the process, we've socked back a little savings.

Consider these supporting statistics in a quote from a recent *Christian Retail* magazine article: "As baby boomers turn sixty, senior citizens will make up a growing percentage of consumers for the next 20 years. Seniors control more than 70% of all disposable income, with $1.6 trillion in spending power and 2/3 of that spent on goods and services, according to 2000 U. S. Census Bureau figures."[1]

I'm surprised they didn't say "*grands* and services." Guess, on the whole, we're more well-heeled than we thought. And who better to spend those hard-earned dollars on than our little darlings?

Let's face it. Nothing's more heartwarming than having the means of introducing grandchildren to new and exciting experiences. In some cases these are things we weren't able to do with our own children, either because of limited income or extenuating circumstances. Sometimes they were simply not interested.

How well I remember the year my husband and I decided our West Coast-cultivated, pre-pubescent boys should explore the Midwestern wilds where we grew up. In order to see other sights and make it a real experience, we routed out a cross-country road trip.

It was an experience, all right.

Once there, they showed sufficient interest. It was the long hours packed in our newly-purchased mini-van that proved the challenge. By the time we pulled up to the Grand Canyon, the last return stop of the two-week trek, both our pocketbooks and patience were spent.

But God is good. Though we had driven through a pouring rainstorm to reach the gorgeous gorge, by the time we arrived, not only had the sky cleared but also the most incredible rainbow I've ever seen arched into its glorious abyss.

"Well, guys, whadda ya think?" I asked in awe.

"Cool," came the collective response. "Can we go home now?"

Needless to say, by the time the grands come along, we've all learned a few valuable lessons about traveling with tots *and* teenagers. Thankfully this allows us more leeway to relive those previously made memories on a more logical level. Or, as it pertains to places we've never been, it provides a completely new experience for the entire family. Either way, it's another of those serendipitous second chances—something we feel is important to do even if it sets us back a pretty penny.

Nor can we escape the fact that life allows only so much time and so many chances to leave—or spend—a legacy. As Rose Kennedy, matriarch of the famous political family, so poignantly put it, "Life is not a matter of milestones but of moments." Perhaps that's why one of our most memorable family forays came shortly after my husband's recovery from five-way heart bypass surgery.

We had long been promising the grands a trip to Disneyland in Anaheim, California, a mere eight hours by car from our home. Heart, almost literally, in hand, Grandpa was determined not to disappoint them. There was no way, though, in light of recent circumstances, that I was going to let him drive. That's how we ended up taking the train and making a matchless memory.

With a total of 14 in tow—the parents weren't going to miss this one!—it actually made twice as much sense. First, it was cheaper than flying. Second, the cushy, oversized seats were well-suited for snoozing, the tables in between great for games, and the kids could run the aisles from one end to the other without worry of them wandering off. Except for Jim and me, it was a new adventure for all, one I highly recommend.

By the way, ever notice how our own grown kids rarely have any serious squabble with us footing the bill for fun? Nor, in most cases, do we, knowing this allows them to spend their stretched-thin savings on other necessities. Still, we have to be careful in our enthusiasm to lead our precocious pack down new and untraversed trails not to leave the impression of having unlimited resources, or to undermine the egos and authority of their parents.

"If kids see grandparents as an unending well of supply," muses Peggy Musgrove, "maybe we have given them sufficient reason to think so."

She tells of the time when they, along with their children and grandchildren, were staying in a downtown hotel that had a revolving restaurant at the top. Their six-year-old grandson, Colin, was asking his dad—to the point of begging—to go and eat there.

"It's just too expensive," his dad stated firmly. Then Colin moved close and whispered something in his ear.

"That's a great idea," the son-in-law laughingly replied. Turning to Peggy and husband, Derald, he spilled the secret. "Colin says we can go because Grandpa will pay."

"We didn't go that time," Peggy says, "because we didn't want to counter his dad's position, but you can be sure Grandpa has paid for many a family outing."

No question—when it comes to money matters, kids can be not only convincing but conniving. In a recent staff chapel, James Bridges, one of our national-level denominational leaders, told the following grandpa tale.

Seems he was recently roaming the game aisle of a toy store with his fifth-grade grandson. Coming upon a particular item, the boy said, "Granddad, my mother told me not to ask you for this game, but wouldn't it be nice if you just thought of buying it all on your own?"

This is the same grandson who, a few years earlier, was told by his father that he and his brother would have to hold his hands if they wanted to walk through the Disney store.

"Dad," he responded, "if you don't mind, I'd like to hold Granddad's hand."

When his father agreed, he whispered in Granddad's ear, "You *did* bring your money with you, didn't you?"

Granddad Bridges admits with a laugh, "It's this kid that keeps me completely aware, as one current popular game show proves, that I am *not* smarter than a fifth-grader."

Seriously, though, sometimes we don't do ourselves, our children, or our grandchildren any favors by stretching the spending too far. We have one dear, elderly friend who relinquished his entire retirement savings attempting to pay his prodigal grandson's way out of trouble. Granted, these are situations that sometimes require the wisdom of Solomon.

In Proverbs 2:8-10 the sage himself guarantees us a guardrail if we'll only take time along the trail to ask God for directions. "He guards the course of the just and protects the way of his faithful ones. Then you will understand what is right and just and fair—every good path. For wisdom will enter your heart, and knowledge will be pleasant to your soul."

Face it. The time comes when we must be looking frugally toward our own future, even letting our offspring foot the occasional bill. This time it's the apostle Paul's teaching in 1 Timothy 5:4 that makes it clear that this is an important part of training, too. "If a widow has children or grandchildren, these should learn first of all to put their religion into practice by caring for their own family and so repaying their parents and grandparents, for this is pleasing to God."

Seems it can be a serious sign of omission—not to mention trouble—if, at the time of life when our children should be caring for us, we're still supporting the entire family.

Along that path, there's some good news. The best trailblazing experiences need not be expensive. Jan Coleman finds she can provide her grands plenty of educational opportunities by taking them to low-priced local sites. Last Christmas, for instance, they visited the nearby historic mining town of Coloma, California.

During one December weekend, the state park dresses up like the 1850s and recreates life during the Gold Rush.

"At first my 11-year-old didn't want to go, but the sights and sounds of the blacksmith shop hooked him. Then he had a ball playing in snow trucked down from the mountains, making a handmade Christmas present for his parents at the nature center, and talking with the 'trapper' in his cabin."

Jan and husband Carl also educated the kids about the Gold Rush era by playing "Imagine if . . ." She freely admits that the best part was how little the afternoon ended up costing.

Another of Jan's grands' favorite frugal things is to spend a morning at their local commuter airport watching the planes come in and out. Even five-year-old Carly loves it.

"Talk about cheap," chirps Jan. "It was free, and it kept them entertained for two hours. They peeked inside planes and talked to pilots." Since almost every sizeable town has an executive airport nearby, this could work in a lot of locales.

Taking this experience to new heights, Jan recently discovered a program called Young Eagles, sponsored by the Experimental Airlines Association, offering free 20-minute airplane rides to children ages 8-17. Geared to giving kids a real up-in-the-air experience, local pilots volunteer their time, asking only that the accompanying adults consider making a donation. More information can be found on the program's web site.[2]

Consider another completely cost-free path we might pursue, that of teaching these fresh new faces how people did things in the "olden" days. How about, say, sharing some silly inherited skills and rough-edged resourcefulness?

For example, I loved showing my grandchildren how my dad taught me to make a whistle from a tree branch and use a comb covered with wax paper for a kazoo. Burning leaves with a magnifying glass was my husband's questionable contribution to our last Camp Gramma, but I have to admit it kept them busy. Me, too—as I ran repeatedly to the back door yelling, "Just don't burn any bugs or set your pants on fire!"

Regarding resourcefulness, it could come as a new revelation to our grandchildren that this is another word for what they now know as recycling. Out of necessity, my grandmothers went green before it became a politically bantered buzzword. For them, this meant keeping baskets full of colorful fabric and tins brimming with buttons. These came from worn-out clothing and were reused for piecing quilts, hooking rugs, and gracing newly made garments. Think this cultivates no current interest? One inherited button tin now sits in my sewing room, where my grands have spent glorious hours sorting through them.

Why, my grandmas even had garbage disposals of sorts. Their food scraps went to feed the livestock or contribute to the garden compost heap for fertilizing.

Though PETA would not be pleased, both grannies were also known to have wrung a few necks in their time—not people's, though at their age I'm sure they had repeatedly encountered the temptation, but chickens'. Many times during my childhood I watched them choose a fat, unfortunate fowl from the flock, firmly grasp its neck, then wind up like a star pitcher. A few flops and feathers later, we had the makings of Sunday dinner.

Admittedly, this fond family reflection is a bit more than many can stomach. Surely we're all glad for more modern and humane methods of food processing. Yet helping our grandchildren understand why people once viewed and did things differently can provide their own eye-opening insight into how things emerge, evolve, and end up on the grocery shelf. Even so, I can't help imagining how my grandmother would cackle now at the thought of chicken's rights.

Two world wars and the Great Depression also caused my parents to be cautious about wasting things. This resulted in an enviable ability to construct things out of almost nothing—a cultivation both their children and grandchildren often benefited from.

One special memory for Derek involves the Halloween my mother fashioned a make-shift superhero costume out of Underoos, a then-popular brand of brightly-colored children's underwear, and an old yellow shirt belonging to Grandpa.

"Just when I thought my brother would have to be a lone Batman," he chuckled.

Then there are the sessions in self-sufficiency. All my boys remember rambling down the rows in Grandpa's vegetable garden, something he loved to tend even after putting in an eight- to ten-hour work day. I especially love Derek's alliterative look back: "Shirtless and sagging," he wrote, "this gray-haired, be-spectacled Buddha would work the corn rows, massaging the dirt the way a seasoned masseuse works the knots from cramped muscles. It seemed, for him, a sanctuary."

A similar insight surfaced on another visit when Derek split his scalp open on the driveway, requiring stitches. Two weeks later, Grandpa insisted he could just snip those stitches out himself. "No sense spendin' money needlessly!"

Again, here's Derek's summation of the experience: "In our current world of expecting convenience and service, he showed me his generation's self-sufficiency." Another memory makes its mark. It also enters the favorite-family-stories hall of fame and is regularly recycled, keeping us all in stitches.

Though our "olden days" are much different than our parents' and grandparents', it's probably equally as astounding to my grandchildren that I lived—briefly—in a time before television. Still, it's good to give them a glimpse into an era when not every form of entertainment required technology, emphasizing that even now some of the best things in life are free and don't need batteries or a link to the Internet. Like every previous grandparenting generation, our underlying hope is that shining a spotlight on the past will provide a clearer path toward appreciating what they have in the present, both materially and spiritually—something we'll illuminate more fully in future chapters.

Conversely, our personal challenge is not to get so caught up in the past that we miss our own opportunities for enlightenment. We can't escape the fact that technology takes a new leap every day. Some of us sages struggle to stay current. That's where our grandkids can teach us a thing or two. For them, breaking new ground on the technological trail is like a walk in the park.

How well I remember being a little leery the first time Liam asked if he could use my computer! After all, there was stuff in there I really didn't want deleted, like a book in progress, for instance. I soon discovered that at age eight he knew a lot more about computers than I did.

"Just let me know when you want me to teach you Power-Point, Grandma," he said smugly as he left that night. Techie little twerp.

These are the times we receive our own revelations, observing not only these little people's patience in helping us find footholds but also how they delight in the reversing of roles. According to an article published last year in our local newspaper, this is one reason inter-generational contact is so important. "Both parties offer a conduit to each other's world," states author Tom McMahon.[3]

I was equally amazed when last visiting our out-of-state grands to discover that 12-year-old granddaughter McKayla's directions are more dependable than most adults'. Besides her talent as a tour guide, the kid's also turning into an organized little list-maker, cell phone texter, and download diva. In her spare time, she excels at gymnastics.

Her brother, Fallon, has likewise plotted a new path, that of becoming a guitar player extraordinaire. How many times did I watch and listen as his fledgling fingers floundered across the strings? Now, after only two years of lessons, he's put together a band. More important to Grandma, he's also accompanying his church youth group's worship team.

By the way, who do you suppose monetarily made both guitar and gymnastic lessons possible? Their other generous grandmother, Lynn. I rest my case.

What fun it is to see our grands grow and begin developing their own skills and abilities! Though we can't claim all the credit for their accomplishments, we can encourage their interests. Once again my gifted and gift-giving friend, Jan, shares how she buys her grandchildren presents for their birthdays and Christmas based on their passions and interests. This year she bought 11-year-old Andrew an art set and sketching paper because he's always drawing.

"He's quite good," says Jan, "so I want to support that."

Seven-year-old Aaron, on the other hand, loves games, something Jan also uses as an opportunity to explore unmarked territory. Her hint is to buy games geared for ages a bit older than the child so that they're challenged to think and learn.

"Just be prepared to take part," she warns. "Now when I come to visit, the younger grands immediately drag them all out. So I sit on the floor and play, even if it means popping an ibuprofen later."

This year Jan plans to teach them more adult card games, just as her grandmother coached her on Canasta when she was their age. When it comes to the grandma game, I would say both hold a winning hand.

Here's where I have to admit to a little grandma envy. Jan is blessed to own a nearby cabin, providing her grandkids a getaway for fishing and fun. Unlike at home, Grandma lets them get as dirty as they want, and they don't have to take showers every night. Worn out as she is by the end of the day, Jan realizes how important it is for her city-bound grandbabies to be in the great outdoors. For them it's a real wilderness experience.

That's not to say you can't have a wild time in the city. My friend Robin is a fairly new grandma who lives in a condo on the 37th floor of a San Francisco high-rise. Her 23-month-old granddaughter Ella's current delight is riding up and down the elevator.

Robin informs me that she simply calls it the 'vator, since everyone already seems to understand that it's "Ella's 'vator."

"Usually we ride it five times up and down," says Grandma Robin, "letting Ella push the buttons. At her age that equals an 'E' ticket on any Disneyland ride."

When it comes to an entrepreneurial educational adventure, author and humorist Martha Bolton takes the prize. What started at Martha's house as her granddaughter's tea shop has now become a full-fledged mall. Seems every summer the grands visit, she adds something new until now there's a beauty shop, restaurant, bookstore, and a whatever-she-can-find-around-Grandma's-house store.

One year Grandma got into the act by purchasing a McDonald's play set that came complete with cash register and food items. That was added to the operation.

You've gotta give the kid credit, though—literally. She's made money out of pieces of paper and even issued everyone credit cards. The restaurant has menus, order forms, and real kid-safe food. She coordinates who works each station by having her cousins, Grandpa, and Grandma fill out "job applications." The others take turns being customers. The "merchandise," complete with price tags, is displayed on TV trays. She hands out receipts and at closing time tapes everything off, placing a sign outside saying when it will be open again.

"I'm not sure what kind of store she'll add next summer," says Martha, "but we're looking forward to finding out!"

The serious side of things is that not only are they all having fun, but it also gives the grands actual experience dealing with "customers" and "running a business.".

"And," Martha adds, "the tea's pretty good too."

Cultural experiences are also important. I recently heard of one grandmother who has made it a tradition to take each grandchild to Europe when he or she turns 13. For most of us that would involve some serious saving.

Thankfully, you don't have to go that far to find culture. Jan exposes her grandchildren by taking them to local live theatre productions, particularly at Christmas. Whether it's the biblical Christmas story or Dickens' *A Christmas Carol*, they enjoy the show, then go out afterward for dessert and talk about it. Last year Jan even chanced taking five-year-old Carly to a local production of *The Nutcracker*, hoping the little tomboy would last through the first act. To Jan's amazement, she sat wide-eyed and entranced.

"That will be our tradition now," says Jan, who bought her a little nutcracker to remember it by.

Again, let me emphasize that those who don't have an abundance of financial resources should never underestimate the significance of the small things we do. Sometimes we forget how many things familiar to us are still mysteries for our grandchildren. In my book *True North*, I tell the story of Liam as a little guy watching me use cellophane tape to mend something. This was a "skill" through years of broken toys and torn pages I had pretty-well perfected. To Liam, though, it was a sticky task yet to be mastered. "Gramma," he said with awe, "you're the best taper in the whole world."

To a child, simply having someone with the time and patience to show them even the tiniest tasks can take on lifelong significance. How many remember the grandparent who taught you to tie your shoes, make cookies, or crochet—or fish, hunt, and throw a ball?

Be forewarned, though. There's no escaping the fact that involving ourselves in our grandchildren's adventures will, like Fallon's guitar, tune us in to their culture as well.

"Friday is dress-up day," Peggy Musgrove's seven-year-old granddaughter, Grace, informed her recently. "Grandpa is always dressed up, so he would fit right in."

Laughing, Peggy replied, "I guess we could just call him a *dressed-up dude*."

"No, Grandma," Grace quickly and condescendingly corrected her. "He's not a *dude*."

"What *is* a dude, then?" Peggy asked.

"Dudes are special t-shirts that say things like, 'I did it but I'm blaming you.'" Though this is likely a current colloquialism peculiar to their locale, there was something about Grace's tone that told Peggy she was probably ignorant for not knowing that.

"So now," says an enlightened Peggy, "I will know a dude if I see one."

Silly or significant, there's no disputing the delight we grandparents get out of taking our grandkids down a few interesting, unexplored trails. From that first exciting stroller ride through the park to a train or airplane ride toward some distant destination, these are experiences we pray will not only educate and inform but also give opportunity for them to sprout spiritual wings, preparing them better for life both here and in the hereafter.

"Start children off on the way they should go," says Proverbs 22:6, "and even when they are old they will not turn from it" (TNIV). Who knows when something we've shown them will come in handy should life take an unexpected turn further down the road? Never was I so grateful for my pioneer underpinnings as when my husband and I ended up living in an isolated Alaska fishing village, teaching me lessons I've elaborated on in my book *True North*.

Most important is remembering that God is the one best able and most wise when it comes to knowing which exposures and experiences our children and grandchildren need. We are but tools He uses to provide opportunities that will open their eyes to life's greater and more gratifying possibilities.

That's why this year we paid for Liam to fly to Idaho to attend church youth camp with Fallon. They had a great time meeting new friends and participating in all the fun activities, but the deepest impact took place during times of hearing God's Word and praying around the altar. For both boys, this resulted in a spiritual odyssey and brotherly bond we could not have orchestrated.

As a confidence-building bonus, for the first time, Liam got to fly home alone. When it comes to leaving an eternal legacy, consider the spiritual symbolism of that.

Psalm 84:5 speaks of those who have set their hearts on pilgrimage. We Christian grandparents are on a journey to our eternal home, blazing the spiritual trail even as generations have before us. What we really want our grandchildren to observe is how we find joy even on the roughest patches of the journey. This means the greatest secret we can share with our grandchildren is how to make the most out of everyday life. "This is the day the LORD has made," Psalm 118:24 declares. "Let us rejoice and be glad in it."

Again, being a grandparent takes us down one of the greatest, most gratifying paths on life's journey. Let's pray we all have a few laps left in us. Trusting God for His blessing of health and strength, let's explore and expose our grands to as many adventures as possible before we reach the end of the trail.

CAMP GRAMMA CLIPBOARD #6

Trying to find unique, creative, and educational things to do with your grandchildren? Maybe even snag a few freebies? Here's some seed for thought:

- Scout out interesting places unique to your particular locale—or theirs, if you're visiting—such as museums, specialty shops, small airports, or food-making factories. Some may offer free or inexpensive tours, even serve up samples.
- Likewise, keep your eyes and ears open for dates and times of special or seasonal events and activities.
- Check to see what programs or classes the local library or community college might offer.
- Do something completely no-cost, like taking a nature walk. Collect pinecones; press fall leaves between wax paper; visit a daffodil, tulip, or wildflower farm; make a snowman; identify local birds and wildlife.
- Share any interesting collections you may have, telling where each piece originated, how it was made, and so on.
- Blaze the trail by being the first person to call and sing to your grandchildren on their birthdays. Describe to them what a special day it was when they were born, who was there, and what happened.
- Each time the family's together, make an express photo studio appointment for an updated or funny picture. During "Summer of the Monkeys," a life-size inflatable chimp became part of our family picture.
- My friend Judy Rachels tops that! Each year she costumes her grandchildren as characters in the Nativity and has a picture taken for the front of their Christmas card.
- For Valentine's Day Jan Coleman buys her grands gift cards to a local book store, then takes them for a Grand-

ma's Day Out to choose something. In this way she cultivates in them her own love for books. A grandma after my own heart!

- Do your own version of Martha's mall (described in this chapter) to help teach business skills, or arrange to tour an actual business—any place that might plant an entrepreneurial seed.

7
Over the River and Through the Woods

I thank my God every time I remember you.
—Philippians 1:3

I had just begun the cool-down exercises at my local women's workout center when something sparkly caught my eye. At first glance it looked like nothing but a fleck of glitter against the gray carpet, yet with each bob and bend the glint seemed to grow. So did my curiosity. On the final flex, I picked it up. To my amazement, it was a tiny diamond, undoubtedly dislodged from someone's ring.

In case the owner came back to claim it, I left it with the equally amazed attendant, then marveled all the way home how such a small stone could sparkle. I could only conclude that the intricately cut facets somehow compensated for its size.

Likewise, those who grandparent from a distance—whether geographically or circumstantially—should never underestimate how bright or enduring their short-term or limited influence may be.

When a friend's daughter moved 500 miles away, she couldn't help but wonder, *Will this relegate me to having only a token role in my grandkids' lives?* Not at all. Whether literal miles or an extenuating circumstance has caused the chasm, there are still ways of staying in touch and having a positive, lasting influence.

As pastor-author Richard Exley reminds us, "God has a history of using the insignificant to accomplish the impossible." When Martha Bolton was growing up, her grandparents lived 2,000 miles away. One best memory from their annual summer visit was of her grandfather taking her for walks in the field behind their house to pick flowers or berries. "It cost him nothing except time, but I will never forget it."

Sadly, I remember very little about my mother's mother, because she died when I was only seven. The mental image I have is of a frail elderly woman, irreversibly bedridden because of a broken hip that didn't mend and several small stokes. Fortunately, a more positive picture superimposes itself: that of me playing on her bed as a child, seeing her sweet smile and pleasant disposition despite the physical pain and confining circumstances—not to mention her infinite patience with an energetic, bed-bouncing little girl—something undoubtedly developed through pain and perseverance.

My brother, James, is enough older to remember her when she was more active and often cared for her many grandchildren. "If we didn't mind her," he reminisced recently, "she could wield a mean maple switch. Sometimes she'd even make us cut our own!"

That sweet little old lady? The thought of such feistiness filled me with unexpected delight. Seems there had once been more to Grandma than met my eye.

Also surprising was his revelation that she was known in her day as a "shoutin' Methodist," meaning Grandma could be quite demonstrative as it pertained to spiritual expression. Somehow over the years she had obviously learned to bring it all into balance. My brother concurs that even her strict discipline didn't keep patience and forgiveness from being two of her most-remembered characteristics as well.

What I eventually came to realize was how my own mother's endearing and free-spirited disposition had been shaped by hers. Mine, some say, is like my mother's, making me ponder again that curious, almost mysterious connection grown between generations despite the quantity or quality of time spent together. I only know that almost every picture of them with those sweet smiles reminds me of the love they lavished on me. To me, there's no question about the lasting legacy my grandmother left, short-lived though our time together was. My greatest hope is to be likewise remembered by my own children and grandchildren.

It's amazing how sparklingly embedded the impact and impressions from even short acquaintance or infrequent visits can be. My friend and fellow-author Sharon Souza concurs. Along with her siblings and cousins, she spent every August with her grandparents from the time she was six years old until she graduated from high school.

"It was the highlight of my year," Sharon says.

She recalls canning peaches—a nearly extinct art—and learning a lot of other cooking skills from her grandmother. Her grandma also took Sharon to the church sewing circle, where she taught her how to embroider.

"I still have a pair of her embroidery scissors," Sharon says, reflecting fondly.

What Sharon remembers most, though—especially since she didn't grow up in a Christian home—is her grandmother's spiritual influence, which she describes as "enormous." Similar in spirit to my own "shoutin' Methodist" grandma, Sharon's grandmother, Rosie Gibson, was a fiery preacher of the Pentecostal persuasion who, during those days, still had health and energy enough to pastor several small churches. Though modern mainline theologians might reckon this a radical role, perhaps they would agree that "radical" is often what's required to leave a lifelong impression on a short-term basis.

"I'd go with them on Saturdays to clean the church for Sunday services," says Sharon, "and she would talk to me about Jesus. There would always be a twinkle in her eye, because she so loved sharing the gospel."

Sharon also remembers her grandmother as a faithful woman of prayer. "I know it was her spiritual influence and prayers that kept my heart open to the Lord long before I came to know Him in a personal way. She could be stern, for sure, but when I think of her I always remember her laughing."

Guess our grandmas had quite a *lot* in common.

Perhaps seeing that constant smile is what makes Sharon so sure that all the dimples in her family originated with Grandma Rosie. Yet deeper than those dimples is the eternal impact she had on Sharon, who, also an author, now serves alongside her husband as a home-based missionary. These grandparents, until their deaths, remained two of the people closest to her—all stemming from that annual summer excursion.

Speaking of summer stays, these varied geographical visits can be an experience and education all on their own, especially when this includes some unanticipated climate changes. On one such visit, my boys remember heading happily for the public pool on a sizzling Kansas summer day, only to be driven out by a sudden thunder and lightning storm. This is a common Midwestern occurrence for which they had no frame of reference—coming first from Alaska and then California. Seeing sunshine one minute and sheets of rain the next, they got caught one day while making a quick grocery run in what Grandpa called a "gully-washer." This resulted in their having to push Grandpa's old gold Matador home after it stalled on a flooded street. That made quite an impression!

I wonder. Could this have given them their first metaphorical model that life as well may be prone to sudden storms, even cataclysmic changes? Then what? Grasping Grandpa's example, there's nothing to do except pray, push hard, and go with the flow.

Fact is, the very houses far-away grandparents live in can conjure up some quaint yet comforting observations, even solidify an unspoken life lesson or two. My oldest son, Damon, remembers my mother taking him up the attic ladder to look in an old trunk containing mementos she had kept from my growing-up years.

That was not only his initial introduction to the benefit of having extra overhead storage but possibly the first time it ever occurred to him that his mother, too, had once been a child.

Seeing how Grandpa added a family room onto the back of their house may also have seeded his lifelong interest in building things. Today he's quite proficient with tools—something he must have inherited since his own dad freely admits it wasn't learned from him.

Then there were the culinary recollections—watching Grandpa pop peas right out of their pods with his pocket knife, hauling in his huge homegrown tomatoes, and husking corn on the cob. Again the question comes: Could this early introduction to garden-fresh edibles be what inspired a cooking interest in all three boys, even culminating in our youngest son's recent graduation from chef's school? No surprise, either, that they picture their grandma—and me, for that matter—always in the kitchen. Someone, after all, has to process all that produce.

Going to their other grandma's was a far different experience. A long-time widow, she lived in a mobile home covered wall-to-wall with knick-knacks. So small was the remaining space that on combined family visits, the cousins were sent to sleep at their great-aunt Rachel's. By contrast, her home was a large old two-storied affair that had the second floor sealed off to save money on utilities.

Now I ask you, what normal kid could resist sneaking up there just to have a look around? To this day my boys swear they slept in a room where someone supposedly died.

Equally as spooky to Derek was the day he spied Grandma's false teeth soaking in a glass next to the sink. If there was any unspoken message, it was probably the importance of dental hygiene—a good thing, since he was the one who eventually required braces.

Another lasting impression is how these people who live far away and aren't your parents will instantly lay aside whatever they're doing should you get hurt. This was something our accident-prone offspring tested almost every trip, resulting in more than one mad dash to the emergency room. From Derek's stitches to Dustin somehow getting a pebble deeply embedded in his knee, every medical emergency found Grandma hovering while Grandpa humored. Doing so, they exhibited two of the most common ways people cope with injury or adversity. Years later, when their grandparents' own health headed downhill, our boys had many heartwarming opportunities to reverse that role.

These visits will also inevitably reveal some ingrained preferences, prejudices, and propensities—things most prone to surface when people are observed in their own element. While Grandpa would permit the purchase of several fruit-flavored soda pops, he stubbornly allowed only one brand of cola in his house—Coca-Cola. That other stuff was just "too sweet." Guess what Dustin's current favorite cola is.

Even the grandest of the grandparents can exhibit unexpected flaws and foibles when their guard is down. Take, for instance, the day some youngsters ran out in front of Grandpa's car, causing him to swerve and sputter a less-than-illustrious misnomer. Oops.

Conversely, the boys' paternal grandmother was, for reasons too complicated and space-consuming to explain, a mass of insecurities, often resulting in loud and hard-to-handle harangues. But, boy, did she love to play board games—as did Dustin! Problem was, she would get mad when he won. Though encouraging competitiveness, her example didn't do much toward instilling good sportsmanship.

While some memories are made of experiences not necessarily laudable, these are experiences that allow grandchildren to make astute observations—even if it requires immediate explanation or correction so they *don't* end up being emulated.

Not to be discounted is how trips to a grandparent's house may positively allow for creativity and exposure not always encouraged at home. Our "adopted" daughter, Karissa, remembers how she and her cousins were permitted to put on Grammy's make-up, thus getting their first experimental introduction to that glamorous part of the grown-up world. Besides her face, Grammy also painted dishes and magnets, implanting an early interest in Karissa to explore and develop her own artistic talent.

"Whew!" someone may be saying about now. "Why the long march down memory lane?" Hopefully, these stories serve to illustrate how even sporadic memories gathered over a gamut of years eventually combine to form a complete picture of the people we know as grandparents. Usually, in fact, it's only as the children and grandchildren age that their frame of reference expands, allowing these reflections to congeal and reveal their deepest overall import. The hoped-for result is that they recognize the rich tapestry that has been woven into their lives, introducing color, texture, and a treasury of golden threads.

For that reason alone, grandparents who get only an occasional glimpse of their grands should make every effort to insure that even short visits are special and therefore significant. Like the preceding illustrations, often it takes is just one or two good memories to form a positive overall impression.

Now imagine having your grandchildren living on another continent. That was the situation for Alice and Elmer Kirsch, whose son and family served several four-year terms as missionaries in far-away Africa. "We tried to keep in frequent touch," says Alice, "so the children would know who we were and that we loved them."

Seems it amounted to much more than that. One of the ways Alice did this was by sending cards, letters, and photographs to the home mailbox, which the kids raced to check out each day. At one point, her youngest grandson, Matthew, had spent several days sick with a fever. When they put him to bed one night, he kept talking about checking tomorrow's mail, certain there would be something from Grandma. Sure enough, though Alice always sent three individual items at a time, miraculously that day only one card arrived, and it was addressed to Matthew. In this way, he knew that not only Grandma loved him—God did too.

Alice also tried to send a box every month or so containing things unavailable in Africa that the parents told them the children were interested in or hungry for. These often included videos taped from TV that kept them up on favorite programs and new products via the commercials. Not surprising, many of their requests were for things they saw advertised, like M&M candies. "While these usually arrived in good shape," says Alice, "once they opened a box to find an M&M explosion."

Another time, the older grandson, Scott, got into a box of paints and within minutes had paint all over him. That's when his mother remembered a second box Grandma had sent containing "crayon soap." Mom popped him in the tub with those, and he had a great time while she hid the paints. "That soap saved the day, his clothes, and my patience," she informed Grandma later.

In order to see the grandkids more than once every four years, the older Kirsches made a visit or two to Africa. It was after one such visit that their grandson Scott became overly anxious about getting back to America. Since it's difficult for children to comprehend time and distance, his parents tried to help by telling him that they would be going back when he turned six in October. When his dad put him to bed that night, Scott announced, "Tonight I'm going to sleep a long time so that when I wake up I'll be six!"

No wonder the overriding emphasis gleaned from stories gathered from long-distance grandparents is the importance of being intentional about keeping in touch. After all, anything built to last takes time and effort, but especially relationships.

Surely this technological age has made it easier than ever to get acquainted and keep our faces in front of far-away family. Naturally, between visits there will be phone calls and e-mail. Some, like our Barcelona-based missionary friends Dan and Kathy Stump, have now installed webcams on their computers. This provides not only a talking tool but a live picture link spanning the miles from Spain to Pennsylvania, where their two darling granddaughters reside.

Those who are less computer-literate, take heart. There are many tangible, less-technical ways of establishing our identities—especially important when our precious prodigies are mere pups.

Consider one idea coming from another California grandma, Carolyn Gilbert. When her granddaughter Izabella, who lives in Florida, was one year old, Carolyn worried that the opposite-coast inconvenience would not allow Izabella enough opportunities to know her and her husband, Larry. That's when an experienced grandma friend, Edna, presented them with a framed photo of themselves.

"She told me to send it to Izabella," Carolyn says, "so that when we talked on the phone, her mom and dad could point to the picture." The hope was that by keeping their photographed faces in front of her, she would make the connection when they eventually came to visit.

It worked.

"What a wonderful feeling it was to walk into their home and have Izabella recognize me right away!" gushes Carolyn.

I did a similar thing with our off-in-Idaho grands when they were younger. Each time I sent a card, I would draw stick figures near the place where I signed our names. Then I would take old snapshots and cut out only our faces, pasting them on top of the stick figures so they could see which grandma and grandpa sent the card. Once or twice I even included pictures of our pups, hoping they would make the canine connection as well.

Speaking of signing cards, here's another sweet story from Alice Kirsch. Seems that when she signed her name on the grandkids' cards, she would always put two Xs inside a circle—a little sign so they would know it was from her. One day grandson Scott asked his dad, "Doesn't Grandma know about hugs? She only puts kisses in my letters." Alice responded right away, letting Scott know that the circle *was* a big hug *while* she gave him two kisses.

At a recent women's retreat I met Linda Mendoza, a gal whose business is taking stick figures to a high-tech level by producing computerized memory books.[1] What this requires is collecting some photos and writing a corresponding story. These are then computer-scanned and -pasted, using a specially produced program to arrange it all. Finally, everything is sent electronically to a consultant who professionally prints and publishes copies of the finished product for each member of the family. I especially loved the sample book one grandma had created titled *Grandma Was Once a Little Girl, Just like You.*

Jan Young, another lady I met at a retreat, took a different electronic route. It started first with e-mailing her two granddaughters, even when they were little and could hardly spell. Their mother would let them write their responses phonetically until they got older and their spelling improved. Jan would also send electronic greeting cards and notes.

Then one of the granddaughters was given a Webkinz—a stuffed animal that actually has its own Web site where one can enter a special code and access a virtual pet to play with.[2] Upon hearing this, Jan decided that she would get one, too, so she and the girls could not only stay in touch electronically but could also interact online.

"We have played for hours," she reports, "just visiting each other's 'rooms' and playing games."

According to Jan, such interactive programs also provide a great way to relate to your grandkids on another level, because they get so excited about sharing all they know. This creates a connection that's a lot more than just electronic.

"The same could be said of anything kids are really into, Jan advises. "I love finding fresh and new ideas as the girls grow older."

I can just hear my grandmother saying, "Mercy me—who could've ever imagined sech a thang!" As a still somewhat computer-challenged grandma, I, too, dub this a bit daunting. Yet it goes to show how far we'll stretch our brains and bodies to stay in touch when separated from our grandbabies.

In addition to e-mail, Jan Young mails monthly care packages, their contents often corresponding with the time of year: school supplies or clothes money in September, fun fall things in October, Thanksgiving tidbits in November, and so on.

This past Easter she sent *herself*. Hopping on a plane to Chicago in order to help her daughter during the girls' spring break, Jan was able to make some extra special memories.

"We went to the park and pretended we were being chased," Jan recalls with a laugh. "By playing down on their level, it gave me an opening to talk about how God protects them." Yet another good example of taking every opportunity to drive those spiritual stakes a little deeper.

Jan Coleman was a long-distance grandma for eight years and always brought a suitcase filled with crafts. "They couldn't wait for me to come!"

Hers, too, were often calendar-coordinated. One Valentine's Day they made placemats using construction paper, stickers, and original art. When finished, they put clear adhesive shelf-liner on both sides to make them reusable. The real lasting value was how this kept Grandma Jan close to their hearts—and tummies—for months afterward.

No doubt about it. The challenge of making memories across the miles can seem monumental. Yet there's an even greater grandparenting gauntlet—that of being right around the corner yet separated by miles of misunderstanding or extenuating circumstances. Then it's not merely a matter of traversing a river or two, but working your way through a thick forest of feelings.

Kathi Macias's middle son, Michael, was barely 17 when he and his 19-year-old girlfriend, Theresa, presented Kathi with her first grandchild, Shana. Being so young, the parents decided not to marry, so Theresa raised Shana pretty much on her own. Michael stayed involved as much as the strained situation would allow but eventually married someone else and had two more children.

Though Kathi lived close enough to see Shana occasionally, she knew something extra was needed if she was to remain a part of her life. So even before Shana could read, Kathi began sending her cards, notes, and pictures once each week.

"I never missed a week," says Kathi, "even when I was on the road or sick."

She has done the same for Brittney and Tyler, her youngest son's children who no longer live with him and, consequently, she also seldom gets to see. Though they're now 16 and 8 respectively, Kathi continues the weekly notes. When signing them, she always reminds her grandchildren how much she loves them but that Jesus loves them even more.

"I don't fully know yet how God will use this weekly investment of a few brief moments," says Kathi, "but I believe it will be worth it in the long run."

I would say it already is, considering that Tyler, in particular, is proud enough of these notes, cards, and photographs to save them in what he calls a "grandma file."

As for Shana, she is now 21 with a brand-new baby of her own and still stays in touch with Grandma Kathi. Sparkle on, sis!

In the case of my friend Norma, for the last few years her grandma's heart has been tugged in two different directions. For reasons she and husband, James, still don't fully understand, their son, soon after marrying, suddenly cut himself off from the family. For Norma and James, who many years earlier had lost a young son to a devastating disease, this was like opening an old wound.

Though difficult enough not to be welcome in their son's home, when they learned he and his wife were expecting their first child, it became almost unbearable. So much did Norma desire to be part of this pregnancy that she would buy baby things, only to return them within a few days, heartbroken at having no hope of offering them. She wasn't even invited to the baby shower.

Unknown to them, God was already beginning to build bridges. Not long after, Norma learned that her nearby married daughter was also expecting. This provided a positive new focus, giving Norma her unrequited grandma "fix" and an opportunity for real hands-on involvement. Soon after birth, Norma was caring for her daughter's baby one day a week in her newly decorated nursery-that-was-once-a-guest-room.

Then, like road markers diminishing the distance, one miracle began to follow another. First, Norma and James finally received an invitation to come and meet their older granddaughter. Then, within months, God used James's more-than-miraculous comeback from a near-fatal cardiac arrest to crack the door of communication with their son. Now, less than a year later, as suddenly as it closed, that door has swung wide open. He has now reestablished his relationship not only with his family but also with the Lord.

At his request, he and James now meet weekly for Bible study. "It's so exciting," Norma told me recently, "to have him tell us about something he's just read in the Bible.

Through it all, my dear friend served as another sparkling example of letting God's love shine across not only miles of misunderstanding but also through that dark forest of our deepest distress.

For any reader who relates, here's some encouragement. Whether the miles are geographical or emotional, one thing no one can be separated from is God's love. "I am convinced," writes Paul in Romans 8:38-39, "that neither death nor life, neither angels nor demons, neither the present nor the future nor any powers, neither height nor depth, nor anything else in all creation, will be able to separate us from the love of God that is in Christ Jesus our Lord." Whatever constitutes the distance between us and those we love, we can trust God's love to help us bridge the gap. With prayer, effort, and a little creativity, a special bond can still be nurtured with our grandkids that surpasses any earthly or emotional obstacle.

CAMP GRAMMA CLIPBOARD #7

In addition to the ideas already recorded, here are some taken from a local newspaper article to help long-distance grandparents cope and keep connected.[3]

- Pack up and send some toys that the children have played with at your house so they'll still feel a connection. Keep some, of course, for their visits.
- Buy a small photo album and take photos of the family and things around your house the children were fond of—your pets, flowers in the garden, or friends they might have played with while there. Write captions under each photo.
- Make digital audiotapes or videotapes or CDs of you singing or reading storybooks. You can even mail the book along so that if the children are old enough, they can follow the words as you read. You can also record personal messages, riddles, and jokes. If you don't own a videocamera, try to borrow or rent one.
- Make the most of the Internet, exchanging e-mail and sending interactive greeting cards. Many free greeting card web sites are available.
- Continue to periodically send photographs, including those of them and you taken together.
- Gifts will surely help keep you in your grandchildren's thoughts, and they don't have to be expensive. Even if you aren't handy with crafts, you can make simple things that appeal to children.
- Phone calls, of course, are always important. Even if your grandchildren are too young to carry on a conversation, they aren't too young to listen.
- Remember—"out of sight, out of mind" is true only if you let it be.

Here are a few additional ideas from Alice Kirsch. While her grandchildren lived in Africa, she—

- sent them personalized story tapes that had their names inserted. A big hit!
- made sure a package arrived a month before Christmas with 25 small Advent boxes, one to open each day until Christmas, so they could have something to look forward to each morning.
- made special outfits for them, like a bride's ensemble for Megan and a cowboy costume for Matthew. This included chaps and boots that he wore every day even when they got too small.

"No wonder," adds Alice, "that every time they went to the post office, they expected to get a box. When they did, they often got so excited their dad would videotape them opening the boxes, even when it wasn't Christmas."

8
Survival Skills

I have been reminded of your sincere faith, which first lived in your grandmother Lois and in your mother Eunice and, I am persuaded, now lives in you also.
—2 Timothy 1:5

Ever since she was a kid growing up in California, my nephew James' wife, Jenny, has eagerly accompanied her dad each summer to a remote fishing camp in Alaska. More than mere recreation, this involves some serious work in potentially dangerous surroundings. She loves it. Two summers ago she decided one son was now old enough for the adventure. His Grandma Carol, who has never set foot in Alaska, was understandably less than thrilled.

Though she didn't say so, her torturous thoughts could easily have included *What if he gets eaten by a bear?* In the end, she had to trust that the survival skills taught by the grandfather to the mother would now be passed along to the grandson. How else, after all, does a kid learn to make it in life? And who better to teach these lessons than a grandparent who's lived through a few wilderness experiences of his own?

Campsites are great teaching grounds, providing a modicum of security while stressing safety. There, surrounded by unfamiliar territory, life's basic building blocks—dress appropriately, take along enough food and water, be aware of your surroundings, never wander off alone, anticipate the unexpected, seek shelter from storms, have the right equipment—take on a whole new dynamic.

Every parent or grandparent who puts out money for camp hopes the kids will learn these lessons while at the same time developing self-confidence, social skills, and spiritual concepts. We rarely consider that they might be picking up pointers that, under unexpected circumstances, could mean the actual difference between life and death.

In the rash of terrible tornadoes recently ravishing our country, a story surfaced about one that struck a Boy Scout camp. When interviewed afterward, several scouts told how putting into practice the skills they had learned had actually saved their fellow scouts' lives. This illustrates the importance of survival skills being engrained, so they can be called up should the situation warrant.

Truth is, it takes all of us a while to learn that life can unexpectedly take some rough routes and disorienting turns. Without survival tools, it's easy for anyone to lose his or her way, but it's especially treacherous in life's winter seasons. Thank goodness for the generations of parents and grandparents who have lived out some cold, hard times and can teach us a thing or two. Many have survived situations we hope never to face.

Jan Coleman reflects on her grandmother as a strong woman who fought many battles in life. After grappling with the Great Depression, she then prayed as her only son was shipped off across the English Channel on D-Day, ultimately fighting the Nazis all the way to Berlin. Meanwhile, she survived emotionally by organizing scrap drives and a neighborhood "victory garden."

Besides the bits already broached, my family members, too, tell tales of living through tough times: hard-pan farming; selling Watkins products from a mule-drawn wagon; working on the railroad; building their own houses; Mom washing my brother's one-and-only pair of overalls every night so he would have clean school clothes; a disastrous dabble in real estate; a short leap at being landlords; moving into a remodeled mortuary; and owning a barely-able-to-pay-the-bills grocery, just to name a few. That doesn't count the illnesses, personal losses, and near-death experiences.

Even during peacetime and under normal circumstances, some severe storms and seasons come with life's territory. Thank God that some of our ancestors survived to share their collective wisdom, helping to prepare future generations for whatever the trail ahead might hold.

The question is, how does one go about passing on these tools? Again, much comes from modeling, our lives alone a testimony to endurance and overcoming. Sometimes survival comes down to simply sticking it out.

Star Richardson's grandmother was a devoted wife, mother, and grandmother who found the Lord early in life and had a firm spiritual foundation. Unfortunately, the man she married had been orphaned early and was left to be raised by alcoholic relatives. Consequently, he became convinced that drinking was easier than dealing with problems, resulting in some rough early years in their marriage. Still, Star's grandmother loved him and was determined to show him God's love.

"She truly lived the life of Christ before him," Star says, "and took her marriage commitment very seriously."

Influenced by his wife's example, he eventually embraced faith. On his deathbed, he told Star that "Nonnie" was the best Christian he had ever known.

"I'm not sure over the years whether anyone encouraged or discouraged her," Star says. "She was just a very strong woman of faith, all about commitment to Christ and her husband."

Star also remembers how she invested much of her life into her grandchildren, faithfully praying for them while truly walking out her Christian life under these extremely difficult circumstances. It made its mark. Today Star wears her grandmother's wedding ring as a reminder of that sparkling example.

Judy Thompson, too, credits her paternal grandmother for sticking with a husband who was not a happy camper. "He hardly talked," Judy told me, "which was good, because when he did it was never nice. The difference between my two grandfathers was that I couldn't get close enough to one or far-enough away from the other."

Struggling at the time with her own major marriage problems, Judy once asked her grandma, "Why didn't you leave him?"

"I never learned to drive," she quipped. "Maybe if I had, I would have left years ago." Seems she did achieve a helpful sense of humor.

In actuality, her grandmother knew more than anyone about the horrible mistreatment Judy's grandfather had received from his own father. Only because of her compassionate, unconditional love did he show his wife a softer side. Herein lies another lesson. Taking the time to understand why people act the way they do can often help us handle an otherwise overbearing, even unbearable, individual.

This made such an impression on Judy that, as a last gift to her grandmother, she gathered the courage to visit this grandfather as he lay dying in the hospital. Though still concerned about how he would react, Judy hoped for one last opportunity to speak with him about the Lord.

"Turns out," Judy told me, laughing, "he had become hard of hearing, which meant I had to yell in order to be heard." In the end, her embarrassment was worth it as he finally acknowledged and accepted Christ.

Both these women modeled a still-significant biblical principle emphasized to the Early Church by the apostle Peter: "Wives, in the same way submit yourselves to your own husbands so that if any of them do not believe the word, they may be won over without words by the behavior of their wives" (1 Peter 3:1). Obviously this indicates good behavior.

Sadly, in our modern society, this is a commitment sometimes misunderstood, even maligned by unscrupulous counselors. Certainly submission has boundaries, and no one could conscientiously counsel someone to stay in an abusive marriage. Still, too many today are encouraged to bail out before allowing God time to turn things around.

Conversely, observing those who model bad behavior can be another way some learn survival skills. Anyone who has had a grouchy parent or grandparent will surely *not* want to be that way. A case in point is Judy's own parents, who, despite this negative role model, became wonderful grandparents to her son, Travis.

Even so, Judy remembers one incident that might have taught him, too, how to survive embarrassment. Seems one day during Travis's first year in high school, Judy was delayed from picking him up, so she asked her mom to do it, explaining carefully where she should park and wait. Unfortunately, Grandma couldn't find a parking place, so she decided she had better go track Travis down. Small snafu. In her haste, she had left her hair in curlers. Imagine her grandson's shock when, standing with a group of friends, he saw Grandma marching down the hall wired for sound, hollering his name. Good kid that he is, Travis introduced her to his friends, then quickly exited.

Guess this didn't traumatize him too much. Today he's a personal fitness trainer and has Grandma lifting weights and doing the treadmill. Why? "Because," Travis told Judy, "I want to keep her around for a long time."

Our boys, too, have suffered episodes of embarrassment with their Grandma Braddy who, as mentioned earlier, had some unfortunate, long-embedded personality problems. Suffice it to say, she was a woman who often trumpeted her offenses and medical maladies no matter the audience. We used to jokingly say that you could always tell when picking her up at the airport who she had sat by on the plane. They were the wild-eyed one(s) pushing everyone else aside to get off.

At family gatherings her loudly stated observations and opinions caused the cousins to avoid unnecessary close contact. Neither did anyone wish to sit too close in church due to, let's just say, her exuberant, ear-splitting style of singing.

Yet there has never been any doubt that she loved her children and grandchildren. The sad truth is that she, too, was a survivor of childhood abuse and rejection and permanently carried the scars. Even later, life dealt her some difficult blows. Never fully accepted by family, she finally found in Jim's dad someone who loved her unconditionally. When he died suddenly at an early age, she was left reeling—a lonely, 51-year-old widow who would never remarry.

Amazing, then, that aside from all this, grandson Damon's most remembered Grandma-ism is "I just want you to love the Lord."

His brother Derek put it this way: "She was loud in opinion but equally loud in love. She always came with a kiss, even when a hug or handshake would have been preferred. Knowing that despite her childhood rejection and life of loss she was a woman who never stopped praying for her adventurous grandchildren, who stayed consistent in her message and made no apologies for her faith or family, I now see her not as loud but strong. I respect that."

The reason for such respect is that it shows courage—something the survivors themselves may not necessarily recognize. Why? Often it's an understated courage, born of adversity yet softly inspiring others not to give up. "Courage doesn't always roar," states author Mary Anne Radmacher. "Sometimes courage is the little voice at the end of the day that says, 'I'll try again tomorrow.'"

Undoubtedly someone reading this has similarly struggled—perhaps still is—with some incredibly difficult life issues. You may wonder how you could possibly be a hero or an inspiration to anyone. Hear the words of Florence Nightingale, a war-time nurse dedicated to helping others survive, who once said, "I am convinced that the greatest heroes are those who do their duty in the daily grind of domestic affairs while the world whirls as a spinning top."

By those standards, anyone, even Grandma Braddy, could be considered a hero. Though, at age 87, she recently passed away, her ongoing desire that her grandchildren love the Lord will undoubtedly be her longest-remembered legacy.

Strange as it seems, even a grouchy or less-than-polished parent or grandparent can cause us to rise above our circumstances. Long before I was born, my brother James remembers the time during World War II when, to find employment, our family was temporarily transplanted from Missouri to California. As the new kid on the block seeking acceptance, one day he noticed some boys playing marbles and asked Grandma Witt for five cents to buy some. How could he, a green country kid, know that if a marble went outside the circle during the game, someone else got to keep it? James soon lost all his marbles—no pun intended.

When he told Grandma, she responded with irrational anger—due perhaps to her own unsettled circumstances—telling him that he had better learn to take closer care of things or he would never amount to anything. Guess those burning words only fueled James' determination to prove her wrong. Following many successful years spent in mortgage banking, he now runs his own business. Were Grandma Witt alive today, she might have to swallow those spicy syllables. No wonder that when asked what survival skill he wants most to pass on to his grandchildren, James answered, "Wisdom."

Thankfully there are infinitely more positive ways grandparents provide their grandchildren the tools to overcome poverty, adversity, and fear, encouraging them to be better than they might have been. Through eyes of experience, we're often better able to see that all children have within them the innate ability to improve and survive life. Often all it takes is someone who believes in them, then offers them an opportunity to help themselves.

Dr. Maximo Rossi, educator and former president of Bethany University in Scotts Valley, California, was admittedly a child whose survival and success depended entirely upon this grandmother's willingness to help.

The opening words of his inaugural address prefaced his predicament: "On a sad Dominican Republic morning in November of 1959, a frightened young unwed mother dropped a nine-month-old baby on a grandmother's lap and ran away. She knew that she and the baby would starve otherwise."

As students, faculty and friends listened intently, he quickly made it clear: he was that potentially challenged child.

"Amidst bitter and desperate tears," he continued, "my heartbroken mother left without me as quickly as she had arrived. As a result, like many others before, I have known abandonment, fear, struggle, disappointment, despair, and embarrassment, because some never thought I was good enough. Perhaps this leads some to ask, 'How did you get here?'"

Dr. Rossi then eloquently elaborated how his paternal grandmother not only saved his physical life but also instilled in him the principles it took to be both spiritually and educationally successful as well.

To Max's grandmother it didn't matter where you came from—what mattered was where you were going. "To her, it was never *if* you get there—it was always *when* you get there! She always saw things not only as they could be but also as they ought to be."

Obviously this required her to look past a few things, like the frequent fights and subsequent scrapes Max got into. "Though the other kid was usually bruised and bleeding," Dr. Rossi related with a laugh, "according to my grandmother, it was always his fault. As for detention after school, 'Well, we'll just have to go see this teacher about that!' she would say."

Not only did she persuade Max to believe that because of God he was destined for greatness, but she also made every effort to convince everybody else that this child, although he had arrived unexpectedly, had a divine purpose. Undoubtedly one of the most difficult things Max Rossi's grandmother ever did was send him to the United States at age 11 so he could get a better education. Yet because of her sacrifice and spiritual encouragement, Maximo Rossi not only survived—he thrived.

A similar story comes from Nettie Lankford, who also attests how her Grandma's loving, caring heart literally saved her life.

"Raised during the Depression years," she wrote recently, "my father worked away from home a lot. My mother had a horrible temper, and when she became angry, she beat my brother and me."

When Nettie was seven years old, her grandparents came to live close by. "Though Grandpa wasn't a Christian," she explains, "he faithfully attended church every Sunday with Grandma, who loved God with all her heart."

Soon after settling, her grandma informed Nettie's mother that she and her brother needed to be in church. Out of respect, the next Sunday her mother had them up, dressed, and ready to be picked up. It was Easter Sunday.

"We had never been in church before, so didn't know what to expect," Nettie remembers. "You can imagine my amazement, seeing the women in their beautiful clothes, hats, and gloves. We were so poor that our clothes had to be bought at the Salvation Army second-hand store or be handmade." Yet when the pastor began to preach, Nettie soon forgot about her clothes, becoming concerned instead about what was on the inside.

"He told how Jesus had died for our sins because He loved us so much. Since there was never any love shown in our home, I didn't know anyone could love me that much. When he gave the altar call, I was the first one there, asking Jesus to forgive me."

Nettie was 18 years old before her parents finally accepted the Lord. During those in-between years she spent a lot of time with her grandma, who would sit in her rocker reading Bible stories. She would then place her hand on Nettie's head, praying she would be used by God just like the faithful people in those pages.

Grandma also affected Nettie's future in another way. "She prayed that when it was time for me to marry, God would bring the right man into my life," Nettie recalls.

Apparently none of the guys Nettie dated got Grandma's approval until, at age 22, Nettie met her future husband. "After several dates, my Grandma finally said to me, 'He's a winner.'" Grandma was right; they've now been married almost 54 years. Emphasizing that a grandmother's influence doesn't stop when we grow up, Nettie also credits her grandmother's prayers for helping her produce a healthy baby boy after several miscarriages.

This brings me to another poignant point about survival. The sad reality is that many of our grandchildren don't come into the world under the most desirable of circumstances. Sometimes this causes us to wonder how any of us will survive.

At the time our oldest grandson was conceived, our son's rebellious and cavalier lifestyle was causing us a great deal of concern. We couldn't help but wonder what kind of parents he and his then girlfriend would be or how much part we would even be allowed to play in our grandchild's life.

Thank God, though circumstances didn't totally or immediately improve, having children did serve as something of a turning point for them. It also offered us a much-desired second chance at making an impact in all of their lives. Camp Gramma became an integral part of my determination to be an influence.

Though, sadly, the marriage didn't survive, the hours I spent speaking into my daughter-in-law's life paid off big time. Because of that early introduction to God, today she and our grandchildren are serving Him and regularly attending church.

A similar scenario explains the underlying reason Jan Young was so determined to tackle the challenging high-tech connections with her two granddaughters described in a previous chapter. For them, too, there was once a bad break in the family circuit involving their daughter, Heather, the girls' mother.

Due to some extenuating circumstances, Heather was an extremely hard child to handle. By the time she was a teenager, almost any attempt to bring her into obedience ended in a screaming match. This was especially hurtful, since Jan and her husband, active church leaders, had tried to set a good example in raising their children.

Then one day Jan came home to find Heather had packed her belongings and left. This was the start of Jan's journey through years of remorse, guilt, and hate-laced feelings toward her daughter for the hurt she had caused their family. Eventually, though, the Lord showed Jan the first step toward healing: accepting Heather for who she is—a person with strong convictions, right or wrong. Even so, it took another two years to heal the hurt and pain, during which time Heather got pregnant. This was a crisis God used for good, causing mother and daughter to finally begin talking and, Jan adds, "crying a lot!" Both eventually asked forgiveness from each other and the Lord.

As a result, the relationship not only survived—today they are best friends. Though they've all been through a lot, Heather's 12-year marriage produced Jan's two precious granddaughters.

Only by letting go and determining to love them all unconditionally did the door finally open so that Jan now has freedom to speak into all their lives. She certainly wants to keep it that way. "This is my second chance to do things right," she reiterates. "Sometimes this means going the extra mile. Especially as grandparents, we often want to see God change our children *now*, but it's all about God's perfect timing, not ours."

This brings up another important point. How can we know the right time and way to intervene, spiritually and otherwise, in our grandchildren's lives, especially when their parents—our own children—are not serving God? Consider this little life-saver, found in James 1:5: "If any of you lack wisdom, you should ask God, who gives generously to all without finding fault, and it will be given to you."

Sometimes, of course, life leaves little question. That's when we find ourselves praying not just for wisdom but also for strength.

When my friend Linda Huddleston's mother died at an early age, she, along with five siblings, were taken in and raised by her grandmother. No small chore.

"Though my grandmother worked seven days a week," Linda told me recently over lunch, "she made only 80 cents an hour. This meant that to survive we had to rely on welfare."

Yet it wasn't the welfare that Linda remembers—it was her grandmother's work ethic.

"My grandmother made it clear through her example that we were not *on* welfare," states Linda emphatically, "we were *assisted* by welfare. There's a big difference."

She also remembers two other important things. First, poor as they were, there was always room for one more, which meant her grandmother often took in others who were desperate or down on their luck. Second, church was never an option. At church Linda and her siblings learned the real source of their grandmother's strength and spiritual wealth.

And guess what? Because of her grandmother's example, not one grandchild ever ended up on welfare. That's a survival story you can take to the bank.

In this chapter's opening scripture, 2 Timothy 1:5, the apostle Paul speaks specifically to Timothy, his son in the faith, about how faith is passed forward. In Timothy's case it came first through his grandmother Lois, then his mother, Eunice—both early converts to Christianity. As for his father, Acts 16:1 indicates that Timothy's father was a Greek and apparently not a believer. Surrogate papa Paul then encourages Timothy to keep his own God-gifted faith flame burning—something symbolically bestowed upon him by the physical laying-on of hands. Though customarily this took place in a ceremony conducted by the church leaders, Paul makes it clear that Grandma Lois and Mother Eunice both had some "hands-on" influence behind the scenes.

As some of our previous stories suggest, there are times when, if our grandchildren are to survive spiritually and our family's faith is to be preserved, circumstances leave us no choice but to become physically involved in our grandchildren's lives.

We call it intervention.

This brings me to one last illustration coming from some courageous colleagues in ministry, Kaye and Harley Allen. Like more and more grandparents today, they have recently taken on the task of temporarily raising three of their nine grandchildren. The way it came about is nothing short of a survival story.

The sad chapter of their story started when, at an early age, their only daughter delved into a destructive, drug-related lifestyle. As years passed, Kaye and Harley held out hope that she would turn her life around and come home. Instead, she chose a path leading to complete alienation. She wanted no part of her minister-parents' lifestyle, nor did she want her children exposed to it. Consequently, Kaye and Harley had no contact with their grandchildren during any of their formative years.

Even so, from time to time the Allens would receive a desperate call from their daughter and would do their best to help, always with little long-term success. Then came one final phone call, this time from jail. Facing an extended incarceration, their daughter was now desperately looking for someone to take her children.

Though I'm certain several readers will relate and sympathize, many of us can hardly imagine the difficulty someone far past child-rearing age would have deciding to take on children he or she had never had a relationship with. What's a grandparent to do?

"Sometimes," says author Margaret Shepherd, "your only transportation is a leap of faith." With hardly a second thought, the Allens hopped on with both feet. Believing that those whom

God calls, He equips, they opened their hearts and home to three of these children whom they hardly knew. What God has accomplished through their faithfulness is nothing short of a miracle.

Now two years into this new living arrangement, the children show only occasional signs of stress. The two younger ones are attending church and doing well in school. The older grandson is employed and thriving, though they are still praying for his salvation. For the first time in their lives, these kids have both physical and spiritual stability.

Against such odds, how did Kaye and Harley's reconciliation with their grandchildren take place so smoothly? The ten-year-old grandson summed it up to Kaye this way: "It's like that was our old life, Grandma, and this is our new one." Without realizing it, he had paraphrased a portion of Scripture found in 2 Corinthians 5:17-18: "If anyone is in Christ, the new creation has come. The old has gone, the new is here! All this is from God who reconciled us unto himself through Christ and gave us the ministry of reconciliation."

"They do miss their mom," Kaye confided. "In spite of her poor choices, she truly cares about them, and they are very close."

Now for the real reconciliation miracle. At a recent women's event Kaye told me that, though still incarcerated, her daughter had finally surrendered her life to the Lord and is actively engaged in church services and Bible study. During a recent phone call to her kids, she informed them that the mom who will soon be coming home will be totally different from the one who left, so be ready.

Kaye could hardly contain her joy. "We believe we're finally living our miracle."

Certainly, with God's help the entire Allen family has survived some spiritually testing times. They are a living testimony to what the apostle Paul wrote in Romans 8:37: "In all these things we are more than conquerors through him who loved us."

Some of us are still facing circumstances that cause us to feel we're fighting not only for our grandchildren's survival but our own as well. At times we wonder if we'll live to tell the story. For those who are currently going through some similar tough times, let me share two profound statements Kaye recently e-mailed me: "The sins of our children are actually a part of the influence we have, and in that there is redemptive value. When you realize that sin is the stuff of which 'all things work together for good,' we can relax and look for the good in our kids rather than wringing our hands over the sin!"

So how do we survive in the meantime? We remain in God's Word, stay on our knees, and keep showing our grandchildren the stuff we're made of.

CAMP GRAMMA CLIPBOARD #8

Looking for practical ways to provide your grandchildren with skills to help them survive emotionally, physically, and spiritually, whether day-to-day or in an emergency? Offer to help:

- Provide lessons that build self-confidence, such as in music, sports, or the arts.
- Send them to camp.
- Enroll in a class teaching emergency first aid and lifesaving techniques.
- Compose a "What would you do if . . ." list that prepares them to avoid or deter dangerous situations.
- Make sure even small children know how to dial 911 and give basic emergency information.
- Give them an opportunity to verbalize their fears and frustrations.
- Share scripture that assures and instructs them of God's help and protection, such as—

    Psalm 46:1: "God is our refuge and strength, an ever-present help in trouble."

    Psalm 121:1-3 "I will lift up my eyes to the mountains—where does my help come from? My help comes from the Lord, the Maker of heaven and earth. He will not let your foot slip—he who watches over you will not slumber."

    Ephesians 6:13-17: "Put on the full armor of God, so that when the day of evil comes, you may be able to stand your ground, and after you have done everything, to stand. Stand firm then, with the belt of truth buckled around your waist, with the breastplate of righteousness in place, and with your feet fitted with the readiness that comes from the gospel of peace. In addition to all this, take up the shield of faith, with which you can extinguish all the flaming arrows of the evil one. Take the helmet of salvation and the sword of the Spirit, which is the word of God."

9
Leaving a Light On

> *Your word is a lamp to my feet and a light to my path.*
> —Psalm 119:105

"Hey, Dad," Judy Hopping's six-year-old grandson, Ricardo, reported after Sunday School one day, "did you know that in Matthew chapter five the Bible says you're supposed to leave the hall light on at night for your children?"

Huh?

Where *do* kids come up with these strange spiritual misconceptions? One can only assume that Ricardo's teacher had used the visual of a nightlight in a dark hallway to illustrate this well-known passage concerning the importance of letting our spiritual lights shine. The boy had simply mixed his metaphors. At least he got the reference right, but Ricardo's right in another respect. All the spiritual light-shining we do grows dim if we don't make sure to leave one on for those we love the most.

According to Psalm 119:105, the Bible provides that lamp to their feet and light to their paths. This means the brightest and best nightlight a grandparent can plug in is an early introduction to God through His Word.

First and foremost, we must illuminate the pathway toward accepting Christ as personal Savior. This requires shining an initial spotlight on Romans 3:23: "For all have sinned and fall short of the glory of God." Then it's only a short step to 1 John 1:9: "If we confess our sins, he is faithful and just and will forgive us our sins and purify us from all unrighteousness."

Once done, we joyfully proceed arm-in-arm down the well-lit lane to Hebrews 13:5, which assures us all, "Never will I leave you: never will I forsake you." For anyone, at any age, accepting God's grace and salvation is the ultimate enlightening experience.

Judging from another story I got from Ricardo's Grandma, this is one more concept on which she might wish to make sure he is clear. Seems asking Jesus into his heart was something else the kid—like most things, it appears—took quite literally. When Judy asked him how he knew Jesus was in his heart, he stated without hesitation that he believed if a lion ran out of the woods after him, Jesus would jump out of his heart and protect him.

Oh, for the faith of a child!

So how can we make sure our grandchildren seriously grasp and grow into the reality of their spiritual experiences? The best way is to turn them on to not only reading but also memorizing scripture. "I have hidden your word in my heart," states Psalm 119:11, "that I might not sin against you."

Here's another added benefit: the scriptures we learn earliest are often the ones we remember best. That's an investment our pastor friends, Cliff and Carol Traub, are planning on taking to the heavenly bank.

When the Traubs' divorced son and seven children recently came to stay part-time, it temporarily turned their 1,400-square-foot house topsy-turvy. Grandma Carol, however, is not one to endure disorganization for long. By her own admission, she rules with a rubber rod—firm yet not unloving or inflexible. As much as she needed to reestablish structure and preserve her own sanity, she knew these uprooted little weeds needed it even more. It wasn't long before she had everyone planted.

Fortunately someone had given them a fairly large camping trailer. Parked safely in the driveway, it became the three boys' bedroom. They are fortunate as well to reside in California and have a swimming pool. This means that a large part of the year the kids can basically live outside. It's like camping out, only at home.

"Many nights," according to Carol, "we get two outdoor grills going and cook our meals while the kids stay cool playing by the pool."

Grandma, however, is not satisfied with simply feeding their tummies and boarding their bodies; her real concern is nurturing and stabilizing their souls. That's why at bedtime she often helps them memorize a scripture or two.

"They already know the entire first chapter of Psalms by heart," Carol told me recently, adding with a sneaky smile "which happens to be my favorite."

What a great starting place! When it comes to good versus evil, therein lies some solid theology. I also love the positive word picture verse three paints, especially for that traumatized little tribe of transplants: "He [the righteous] is like a tree planted by streams of water, which yields its fruit in season and whose leaf does not wither. Whatever he does prospers." Because the Psalms are poetic, they lyrically lend themselves to memorization.

Judging from what one of Carol's granddaughters recently told her, a spark has surely been kindled. "Grandma," she whispered, "I'd like this to be our home forever."

Not certain how long this arduous living arrangement will last, Carol has her spotlight focused on a more permanent dwelling place. She believes by instilling God's Word in her grandchildren's hearts, whatever happens on earth, someday they'll all live together forever in heaven. For now that hope keeps her going. That's why she takes every opportunity to flip that illuminating spiritual switch.

Another truth about early biblical teachings is that they can become so engrained we may not even realize it when, as adults, we start spouting scriptural principles. Take, for instance, another portion from the address given by Max Rossi to the Bethany College students, as mentioned in the last chapter. The principles he credits his grandmother for are straight out of Scripture—reinforced, I'm sure, by his own subsequent reading. To underscore the point, I've taken the liberty to insert some supporting passages.

"This journey has taught me many things," Dr. Rossi stated. "I have learned that we must love people and use things [Matthew 19:19; John 13:35]; that we must hold on to earthly things with a very light grip as it is certain that they will pass away [1 John 2:15]; that we must live with the light of eternity in mind [Matthew 6:19-21]; that we should surround ourselves and listen to godly people [Proverbs 11:14]; that if one lacks wisdom, he should ask of God [James 1:5]; that leaders should be swift to hear, but slow to speak [James 1:19]; that it is good to cry with those who cry and rejoice with those who have cause to rejoice [Romans 12:15]; that we must encourage one another [Hebrews 3:13], build up each other [1 Thessalonians 5:11], and forgive one another [Ephesians 4:32; Colossians 3:13] because our battle is not against flesh and blood [Ephesians 6:12]; that Christians must seek to serve, and not to be served [Ephesians 6:7-8]; that every good gift and every perfect gift is from above, and comes down from the Father of lights, with whom there is no variation or shadow of turning [James 1:17]."

See what I mean? It's surprising, too, how an occasional biblical phrase will even worm its way into some secular venue. I recently heard a television commentator refer to someone as the "salt of the earth." Without realizing it, he had used a phrase straight out of Ricardo's earlier Scripture reference. It just goes to show the amazing staying power of God's Word, seasoning even a secular speaker's words.

Obviously those early lessons that served Dr. Rossi well throughout life are, along with others, fundamental facts that none of us are ever too old to learn or be reminded of. This brings another point to light. If we are to teach our grandchildren the importance of knowing God's Word, we need to be reading and applying it daily ourselves. Though the Bible is often the first place we turn when times get tough, wisdom says we shouldn't wait until the lights go out to start searching.

"Everyone who hears these words of mine and puts them into practice," Jesus directed His disciples in Matthew 7:24, "is like a wise man who built his house on the rock. The rain came down, the streams rose and the winds blew and beat against that house; yet it did not fall because it had its foundation on the rock." I've always said that walking on water is easy when you know where the rocks are.

Walking in the dark, however, is a whole different story, something I was reminded of on a recent trip to visit missionary friends in Tanzania, Africa. We had just spent a second day visiting various church projects on the island of Zanzibar when the electricity at our hotel unexpectedly went out. Later we learned this was part of an overall outage affecting even areas on the mainland. Suddenly that oft-quoted camping rule about always carrying a flashlight came blinking back. To our chagrin, none of us seasoned sojourners had one.

Working our way down the dark streets to find a restaurant that night with only the aid of a cell phone beam was an interesting yet somewhat unsettling experience. How relieved we were upon returning to our hotel to discover it had a back-up generator! I wonder—could this be why Africa is commonly called the "dark continent?"

Of course, all you have to do is pick up a newspaper or flip through the television channels to see that our entire planet has become a dark and dangerous place. The stuff our grandchildren are being exposed to daily is nothing short of demonic. Worse are the things we can't see—or foresee. No wonder the best lesson we can teach them is the importance of keeping a power-filled scriptural back-up supply handy. Since Ephesians 6:17 refers to God's word as the "sword of the Spirit," I love telling my grandkids it's better than having a Star Wars light saber.

I suppose someone might say, "Wait a minute. Isn't that why we take them to church—to learn God's Word?" Yes. Yet, like Ricardo, it's obviously very easy for them to pick up some misperceptions. Scarier still is that at some point they may even encounter an intentionally stupid—or simply stupid—teaching or two. Thankfully, this is rare, but it's nothing new. Why else would the apostle Peter, pastor of the first Christian church in Jerusalem, warn his flock of false teachers among them. "They will secretly introduce destructive heresies," he warned, "even denying the sovereign Lord who bought them" (2 Peter 2:1).

Those of us who have been around the biblical block a few times know we must all be careful about accepting any advice or counsel that does not agree with God's Word. The only way we can know is to read it, then make comparisons. Not only may we save ourselves from a dark, destructive detour—we'll also be better able to spotlight the dangers for our offspring.

For that very reason the apostle Paul reminded his young protégé, Timothy, that all scripture is inspired and useful for teaching, rebuking, correcting, and training in righteousness, so that the man [or woman] of God may be thoroughly equipped for every good work (2 Timothy 3:16-17).

Judging from a story stemming out of another of Grandma Judy's visits, this is the same lesson our young friend Ricardo's dad is hoping to impress on his children. Seems following a trip to the store, Judy was returning to her son's apartment burdened down with grocery bags. This made it easy for her second small grandson, Daniel, to slip away from her, make a mad dash for the fire alarm, and pull it. Its immediate and incessant screech was nothing compared to the scolding he got as Grandma hustled him into the apartment. Daniel's dad was beside himself with anger and disappointment that his "perfect" toddler might have actually premeditated the pull. The boy was banished to his bedroom for a time out.

Feeling she shared some blame for not keeping one hand on him, Grandma followed. As she attempted explaining to the toddler the seriousness of what he had done, the bedroom door suddenly flew open, and a Bible was surreptitiously shoved onto the floor by her son. His suggestion was that she read something to Daniel that might help him understand.

Suddenly Judy was at a loss. Where to start? Obey your father and mother? Daniel in the lion's den? Hell is a hot place? She decided that at his age some situations are probably best left to a loose and loving paraphrase.

This brings us to another great thing about God's Word: the older we get, the more scripture takes on its own personal application. Therefore, we need not worry how much immediate impact a particular verse may make. "Train a child in the way he should go," Proverbs 22:6 points out, "and when he is old he will not turn from it." Contrary to the claim of some that this serves as a guaranteed spiritual life-preserver, I see it more as a two-part principle. Our part is to make sure the scriptural seeds are planted; the rest, quite simply, belongs to God. As the Master Gardener, He alone knows the exact season in which to make them bloom.

Consider this spiritual schematic. Like our grandchildren, the Bible is alive and active (Hebrews 4:12). This means that, though most of it has been around for more than 2,000 years, it's constantly current, always carving its pattern into our lives. By committing it to memory, Scripture serves as our conscience for sin, convicting, and keeping us on the right road (Psalm 119:11). As already stated, it illuminates the way, making it easier for us to stay the course (Psalm 119:105). At the same time, it provides food for thought, filling our minds and hearts with both God's complexities and compassion (Psalm 119:97-99). Finally, it is eternal. Jesus said it himself in Matthew 24:35: "Heaven and earth will pass away, but my words will never pass away."

Therein lies our real comfort.

Let's face it. The time will inevitably come when we grandparents are no longer around. Then it may not be enough to have shared our limited wisdom and taught the grandkids every trick we know. They need to be shown how Scripture sheds light on every subject. Like a spiritual refrigerator, every time they open it, something soul-nourishing is illuminated.

In this way they'll also understand that these aren't just our bright ideas, rather, that they originated from a higher source of power. No wonder a grandparent's greatest hope is to get these little live wires turned on to reading God's Word for themselves.

Martha Bolton has come up with a meaningful way of combining both. She and her husband have made a practice of putting God's Word personally in the hands of their grandchildren by purchasing each one a Bible. Grandma then inscribes something especially for them on the inside page.

"It's comforting," Martha says, "to know that for the rest of their lives whenever they're feeling down and reach for their Bible for encouragement, they'll also be reminded of Nana and Grandpa's love."

This last Christmas the Boltons took the personalization to a higher plain. They bought Bibles for each of their sons and grandchildren through an online company with the computerized capability of inserting the kids' names into various scriptures.[1] The Bibles they purchased for their son and daughter-in-law also incorporated each others' names as well as the recipient's hometown.

"We handed them out on Christmas Eve, and everyone loved them," Martha says. "My family was excited just to see each of their names on the front of the Bible. Then, when I showed them the selected personalized scriptures, they were doubly delighted! Even the little ones got a surprise out of seeing their names surface inside."

Like most Christian families, we Braddys have an extensive collection of old family Bibles. Partly it's because I'm not sure what to do with all of them. A few are literally falling apart. Those that are intact I'll certainly pass on to my children; others I'll eventually give away. For now I keep them in an office cupboard, because from time to time I love to peruse their pages.

Old family Bibles represent a rich spiritual heritage. Within them are not only the words of eternal life but also tucked-in treasures representing, in our case at least, the lives of three generations. One I cherish in particular is a New Testament belonging to my Grandmother Witt. Judging from its cover, it must be more than 100 years old, which means it was undoubtedly passed down to her. This makes it even more precious. Though I never knew my grandmother well, or my great-grandmother at all, I have only to open those pages to get a multigenerational glimpse. There I find not only specially underlined scriptures but also pressed flowers, newspaper clippings, and notes. Who knows how old some are? Yet each bit of memorabilia speaks across the years to something of the previous owners' pleasures and perspectives.

Most interesting to me is a short letter and photo my grandmother received from her youngest son while he was stationed in Korea during the 1950s conflict. This leads me to imagine through how many other tumultuous times at least two generations of grandmothers sought comfort in the old Book's pages.

Of course, the real literary legacy is in the reading. Another of my most cherished memories is that of seeing my dad sitting on our living room couch each evening, the lamplight shining on the open Bible in his lap. Surely my parents did their best to teach their children Christian principles. The reflection of this regularly read Book in their lives was what ultimately drew us to its Author.

Thank God for parents and grandparents who, through word and deed, flood our pathways with God's light, showing us the way to keep its life-giving commandments. "My son [or daughter]," prompts Proverbs 6:20-23, "keep your father's commands and do not forsake your mother's teaching. Bind them upon your heart forever; fasten them around your neck. When you walk, they will guide you; when you sleep, they will watch over you; when you awake, they will speak to you. For these commands are a lamp, this teaching is a light, and the corrections of discipline are the way to life."

Perhaps you are the first generation in your family to serve God. What a glorious privilege you have of passing on this new heritage! All the more reason to make sure you hide God's Word in your own heart, then shine it on the path of those trailing behind you.

Truth is, even we grandparents never outgrow the need for a nightlight. If you're like me, many are the sleepless hours I've spent fighting shadowy fears over the physical safety and spiritual well-being of my children and grandchildren. Let me share one way I found to finally rest easy. When praying for your precious protégés, insert God's promises. This means memorizing scriptures that speak of God's love and faithfulness, then making them part of our prayers. How does this help? According to 1 Chronicles 16:15, "He remembers his covenant forever, the word he commanded, for a thousand generations."

Knowing God honors His Word should help us rest assured. It's like a nightlight that casts its comforting glow not only in our souls but all the way to eternity.

CAMP GRAMMA CLIPBOARD #9

Looking for ways of introducing and interesting your grandchildren in God's Word? Consider these.

- Conduct a Bible quiz. Compose a list of general Bible story questions. Have the quizzers sit on chairs and jump up if they know the answer. Or give them a colorful paddle to raise.
- When doing your Bible lesson, allow the kids to look up and read the scriptures for themselves. Even though this takes more time, it will help them familiarize themselves with where to find what we used to call "the address," giving them "ownership."
- Use a flannelgraph or picture books. This helps them visualize what the Bible characters, countryside, and other things might have looked like. Plus they'll enjoy participating by holding and placing these items.
- Conduct a contest on memorizing the books of the Bible. Offer a special prize at the end of the week for anyone who can repeat them in order from memory.
- Do the same using special memory verses.
- Plan your own "Summer of the Spies" by presenting them with the fun things described in Clipboard #1 that will help them scout out biblical "clues."
- At an appropriate age—probably no younger than seven or eight—show or present each grandchild with an old family Bible and a photograph of the person it belonged to.

Want to order the personalized Bibles that Martha Bolton gave her grandkids? Check out the web site at <www.personalpromisebible.com>. Here's additional contact information:

Telephone: 509-627-2607
Toll Free: 866-YOURBIBLE (866-968-7242)
Fax: 775-402-2106

Postal address
Personal Promise Bible
470 Heritage Hills Drive
Richland, WA 99352

10
Bug Spray

> *Surely he will save you from the fowler's snare*
> *and from the deadly pestilence.*
> —Psalm 91:3

Bzzzz. Whirrr. Zzzit. The annoying noise coming from above our bunk in the small motor home was loud enough to wake me and my husband, Jim, from a sound sleep. Groggily I gathered my thoughts. Where were we? Oh, yeah—on a cross-country family camping expedition through the Alaskan wilderness. Turning over to see what was making all that commotion, I was startled awake. Covering the screened vent just above our heads were a million monster mosquitoes. *No wonder they're jokingly referred to as the Alaska state bird*, I remember thinking. Then suddenly it struck me: these blood-sucking "birds" were looking for breakfast. Suddenly a second reality set in.

I had to go to the bathroom.

This meant a mad dash to the outdoor facilities 30 feet away. Eyes now fully open, one thing came clear. If any of us was going to make it back unbitten, we needed protection. Time to brandish the bug spray!

Likewise, in the plagues of life, we must make sure our children and grandchildren are protected—not with bug spray but with prayer. Grandparents are, after all, the ones most likely to slather it on.

Fact is, it wasn't more than a few hours after the itchy episode above—which actually took place when our boys were still quite small—that then-three-year-old son Dustin fell off the monkey bars at a rustic rest stop and broke his arm. Praying all the way, we headed for the nearest hospital—two tortuous, road-twisting hours away—wondering what we would find when we got there. Thankfully, we came upon a clean, well-equipped clinic with a competent, compassionate doctor who set Dustin's arm and soon got us back on our way to Anchorage. Only later did I discover that we weren't the only ones praying.

"So that's why I woke up in the middle of the night with a niggling need to pray," my mother said when I called to tell her what had happened.

No surprise, really. Prayer was something Mom practiced in some form almost every waking hour. She could have been the poster grandparent for 1 Thessalonians 5:16-18: "Be joyful always, pray continually; give thanks in all circumstances, for this is God's will for you in Christ Jesus." Judging from the many stories I received praising the power of praying grandmothers, she is not an isolated example.

Nettie Lankford underscored how her grandma, the same one cited in an earlier chapter for literally saving her life, prayed day and night for her four children. "She wanted to see them all saved and serving God. I'm happy to say she did."

Nettie can remember walking into her grandma's house and hearing her pray specifically for one uncle who was in the Army, stationed in Europe during World War II during some of the fiercest fighting.

"When he came home," Nettie says, "he told my Grandma there were times when he could actually hear her praying for him." Now that's some powerful pesticide.

Likewise my husband's brother, who as a young man briefly took a prodigal path, vividly remembers many nights sneaking home late and hearing his parents, still awake in their bedroom, praying for him. Thanks to those protective prayers, both boys eventually settled down, married, and entered the ministry. But the prayers didn't end there. Over the years Grandma Braddy's prayers spread like a bug bomb, eventually enveloping all five grandchildren.

No question. Hearing someone pray for you makes an indelible impression. It also sets an unforgettable example, especially when God allows you to see an immediate answer.

A few years ago during a holiday visit, my four oldest grandchildren and I took a walk to the park across the street. This ended up involving a daring venture down an unfrequented maintenance road leading to a solitary opening in a concrete safety wall. Behind that ran some railroad tracks. We had walked the parallel path as far I felt comfortable and had just turned back when I saw that our only exit was now blocked by an unmarked pick-up truck. Its scruffy-looking driver was standing outside staring ominously in our direction. Wanting to believe the man posed no threat, but having seen too many scary news stories to be sure, I felt unsettlingly vulnerable. It didn't help to realize we were too far away for anyone to see or hear us. Sensing my concern, the kids got scared.

"Okay, you guys." I summoned my brave voice. "We need to pray and ask Jesus to protect us." We did just that, and, I kid you not, when we opened our eyes the man and his truck were gone.

The grands raced home to share what, in their minds, was nothing short of a modern miracle. I, too, admit being amazed at receiving such an immediate answer. It was newsworthy to be sure, but not the end of the story.

A few months later, my son called from Idaho to tell me about a camping trip he and the kids had just taken. While there, he wanted them to experience their first canoe ride. A terrifyingly tipsy try-out, however, made them more than a little leery. After Dad applied a little parental pressure, they finally conceded to another try. "But they were prayin' all the way, Mom," he told me, laughing, "'just like Gramma did at the railroad tracks.'"

I was truly touched—especially remembering how secretly scared-silly I, too, had been. Perhaps this is what author Dorothy Bernard meant when she wrote, "Courage is fear that has said its prayers."

It all sounds perfectly reasonable, though, when you consider yet another spiritual lesson from Max Rossi's grandmother. "She convinced me that as a son of God I was privileged and the Almighty Heavenly Father always heard the prayers of a child first." Then he adds, "Thank the Lord for a grandmother who not only took me in and taught me the fear of God, but also the value of prayer."

Should anyone think this theory a little far-fetched, consider this. According to Jesus, kids absolutely have an edge. "Let the little children come to me, and do not hinder them," he admonished his disciples in Matthew 19:14, "for the kingdom of heaven belongs to such as these."

You would think the disciples might have already been clear on that concept. Only a chapter before, Jesus stood a child among them, saying, "I tell you the truth, unless you change and become like little children, you will never enter the kingdom of heaven" (Matthew 18:3). He then cited two of the tot's specific virtues: humility and unquestioning faith—two attributes many adults shed as they mature.

Only after observing the consistency and consequent effectiveness of Jesus' own personal prayer priority did one disciple finally make the connection. "Lord," he says in Luke 11:1, "teach us to pray." From this request comes perhaps the Bible's most famous prayer pattern: the Lord's Prayer (Matthew 6:9-13 and Luke 11:2-4). In it, Christ teaches us to acknowledge, first and foremost, who and where God is, seek His will above all else, then make our own needs known.

Maybe that's why when prodding our own little disciples to pray, we sometimes start them off with a "pre-packaged" prayer or two. Take this familiar mealtime model for instance: "God is great, God is good, and we thank Him for this food. Amen." Then there's the infamous bedtime blessing: "Now I lay me down to sleep. I pray the Lord my soul to keep. If I should die before I wake, I pray the Lord my soul to take."

My husband admits having a small problem with this last one when he was a child. "When you're only five years old," he says, "the idea that you might die during the night is a rather scary prospect." I agree. The last thing we want is for prayer to have an adverse effect.

Thankfully, there's a rewritten version that, besides being more closely connected to Scripture, should help kids rest easier: "Now I lay me down to sleep. I pray the Lord my soul to keep. May angels watch me through the night and wake me with the morning light."

Point is, whether memorized or made up, we should never disdain or discount the effectiveness of a child's prayer efforts—even if some come out downright hilarious. Consider a few too-good-not-to-share samples I found via e-mail.

Dear God, wrote Norma, *did you mean for the giraffe to look like that, or was it an accident?* A grateful though obviously disappointed Alex prayed, *Dear God, thank you for my baby brother, but what I really wanted was a puppy.* Taking no chances, Ryan came straight to the point: *Dear God, please send me a pony. I never asked for anything before. You can look it up.*

The following young ladies obviously put some deep thought into their prayers. *Dear God,* Jane queried, *instead of letting people die and having to make new ones, why don't you just keep the ones you have now?* Nan simply wanted to know—*Who draws the lines around the countries?*

Some of the prayers, however, were touchingly poignant, modeling a lesson on honest, heartfelt expression we adults might do well to adapt. *Dear God,* Elliot stated sweetly, *I think about you sometimes, even when I'm not praying.* George expressed his admiration: *Dear God, I bet it is very hard for you to love all the people in the world. There are only four in our family, and I can never do it.* Eugene worded his wonder this way: *Dear God, I didn't think orange went with purple until I saw the sunset you made on Tuesday. That was cool!*

Perhaps my personal favorite, though, comes from Cathy—a kid who obviously has no trouble believing that God not only hears but sees us: *Dear God, if you watch me in church Sunday, I'll show you my new shoes.*

Because kids are so trusting, prayer comes easy for them. Likewise they trust the adults in their lives to take care of them, illustrated by yet another example from our recent Africa expedition. Following our time in Tanzania, we had come to Kenya for one last week of visiting various pastors and projects. As a mid-trip treat, our friends and missionary hosts, the Hansons, scheduled a three-day breather in the form of a fly-in safari at a nearby wild game park. Their entire Nairobi-based family accompanied us, including Grandmas Gloria and Becky, and not-yet-one-year-old granddaughter Sienna. This was Camp Gramma to the max!

To our amazement, she and Mom, Rosemarie, didn't just settle comfortably into camp; rather, Sienna bounced right along with us in the Land Rover over rough roads and cross-country chases. Rain or shine, bugs or water buffalo, she showed no fear. Why? Because one grandma or the other always had her covered. Several times I peeked back to see how she was faring, only to find her slumped on some grandma's lap, sound asleep and tucked securely in a Maasai tribal blanket—the total picture of trust.

And why not? At this stage in life Sienna has no idea of the untamed territory she'll be growing up in—and not only in Africa.

Like many missionary kids, coming back to the States could ultimately be her most unsettling experience.

Speaking of which, isn't finding ourselves in unfamiliar surroundings the very thing that sends most of us diving for cover? All it takes is one eyes-wide-open foray into the real world to realize that not only do pests come in all shapes and sizes, but dealing with unknown, even dangerous, dilemmas is a lifelong process.

Take for instance one last experience from that African expedition. Overindulged American that I am, I had already been a bit disconcerted when told that while on safari we would be sleeping in tents. Imagine my relief upon discovering that these were not puny pup tents—rather, well-appointed, heavy-duty canvas contraptions complete with fans, furnishings, and bathroom facilities. Think *Out of Africa*. Thank goodness they also had floors and zippers, because on the last day I was mobbed by monkeys.

We had been warned that the sneaky snipers were about but hadn't actually seen any. Then on the last morning—having sleepily opted out of a final sunrise safari—I carelessly left some cookies from our morning coffee on a table just outside the tent.

Those impudent little primates considered this an open invitation to brunch! By the time I realized what was happening, snatched the remaining snacks, and zipped myself back inside the tent, word had already spread to a family of friendly warthogs.

For the next hour I huddled inside as my new breakfast buddies either scampered across the top of the tent or snuffled rudely around outside. *Lord*, I prayed, *don't let there be any varmint-sized holes in this habitat.*

Certainly I was depending on the tent for protection, but noticing how thin the covering of canvas was, my real refuge became prayer. I took Psalm 91: 9-10 quite literally: "If you say, 'The Lord is my refuge,' and you make the Most High your dwelling, no harm will overtake you, no disaster will come near your tent" [TNIV].

Imagine the kick my grandkids got out of that story. It also opened an opportunity for me to remind them that there will be times in life when we all need a place of supernatural protection and how prayer provides just that. "You are my hiding place," says Psalm 32:7; "you will protect me from trouble and surround me with songs of deliverance." Even if it's to the beat of monkeys' feet.

Knowing how our families depend on our prayers, one of our greatest spiritual challenges as grandparents is finding a way of transferring that trust to the Lord. One way to do that is helping our children and grandchildren understand the benefits of personal prayer. Something it never hurts to be reminded of ourselves.

First, prayer relieves anxiety. "Do not be anxious about anything," Paul says in Philippians 4:6-7, "but in everything, by prayer and petition, with thanksgiving, present your requests to God." Or as someone once said, "Why worry when you can pray?" Too often, unfortunately, we get that reversed. Yet worry accomplishes nothing positive while prayer puts the power of heaven to work on our behalf.

The next verse tells of the promise attached: "And the peace of God, which transcends all understanding, will guard your hearts and your minds in Christ Jesus" (Philippians 4:7). Perhaps the key to that peace is in the little phrase found in verse 6, "with thanksgiving." Thanking God indicates that we have already received something from Him. And we have. Whether the answer comes immediately or eventually, like Sienna's Maasi blanket, His supernatural peace settles over our hearts and minds. How wonderful to know that even as our prayers cover others, God has us covered as well!

The best news is we are not praying alone. First John 2:1 tells us "We have one who speaks to the Father in our defense—Jesus Christ, the Righteous One." Think of it. Christ is our advocate—or lawyer. Hebrews also repeatedly refers to Him also as our high priest, the only one righteous enough to go before God asking anything. Yet He is undertaking on our behalf.

According to Romans 8:26, the Holy Spirit helps too. "We do not know what we ought to pray for," it states in part, "but the Spirit himself intercedes for us with groans that words cannot express." Been there, experienced that. All, the next verse adds, "in accordance with God's will." What more could we possibly ask?

Even in our human helplessness, James 5:16 assures us that "The prayer of a righteous man is powerful and effective." When we can do nothing else, we can pray. That's not saying, though, that we should pray only when we have tried everything else. Prayer is the most active, powerful, and effective thing we can do.

"But what if there's no time to compose a complete supplication?" someone may say. Then just say, "Jesus." His name alone provides both immediate access and a place of protection. "The name of the LORD is a strong tower," states Proverbs 18:10; "the righteous run to it and are safe." Saying "Jesus" says it all.

Preparing to go to Africa, I discovered one of the most convenient and effective products ever made: bug spray wipes. These small pesticide-soaked sheets can be carried anywhere, allowing us to administer a layer of protection wherever we are. Once applied, it's, as one old deodorant commercial claimed, like having an invisible shield that keeps working even though we can't see it.

Likewise, prayer can be quickly pulled out and administered at any time in any place. My favorite illustration of this is captured in a poem I found tucked inside one of my dad's old Bibles. Written by librarian and poet Sam Walter Foss, "The Prayer of Cyrus Brown" employs humor to make a most serious and assuring point.

> *"The proper way for a man to pray,"*
>   *Said Deacon Lemuel Keyes,*
> *"And the only proper attitude*
>   *Is down upon his knees."*

> *"No, I should say the way to pray,"*
>   *Said Reverend Doctor Wise,*
> *"Is standing straight with outstretched arms*
>   *And rapt and upturned eyes."*

"Oh, no, no, no," said Elder Slow,
 Such posture is too proud.
"A man should pray with eyes fast-closed
 And head contritely bowed."

"It seems to me his hands should be
 Austerely clasped in front
With both thumbs pointing toward the ground,"
 Said Reverend Doctor Blunt.

"Last year I fell in Hodgekin's well
 Headfirst," said Cyrus Brown,
"With both my heels a-stickin' up
 And my head a-pointin' down.

"And I made a prayer right then and there,
 The best prayer I ever said,
The prayin'est prayer I ever prayed,
 A-standin' on my head."

Seems whatever "position" we find ourselves in, as long as we are conscious, we can pray. There's only one place we may find ourselves getting a bit bogged down. That's in the muddy waters of seemingly unanswered supplications. It's something that can present a hard concept for anyone to grasp, but especially for a grandchild like Ricardo, our literal little friend from the last chapter.

One day while cutting up salad stuff, Ricardo's Grandma Judy accidentally sliced a thin layer of skin from the tip of her finger. Being a difficult spot to bandage, she finally gave up and left it unwrapped. As soon as Ricardo noticed the boo-boo, the questioning started.

"Gramma, what happened to your finger?"

"I accidentally cut it."

"Did you ask Jesus to heal it?"

"Of course I did."

Ricardo took another close look. "Well, He didn't do a very good job, did He?"

"This opened the door," Judy told me, laughing, "to a discussion on instant healing versus healings that take longer versus healings that may only occur when we get to heaven." Then she added honestly, "None of which were of any interest to him."

When these difficult dilemmas surface, one way of interesting our grandchildren without confusing them is to illustrate with something simple they relate to. In this case, we might remind them that God can't be approached like a fast food drive-through window. To God every prayer is like a special order, meaning some take longer than others. Even then, things may not come out exactly as we had hoped. Sometimes we simply have to take whatever God puts on our plate, trusting it will be good for us.

Trust, of course, is not a trivial matter. Who doesn't sometimes struggle when seeing situations that, no matter how hard we pray, remain unimproved or seem to worsen? Hopefully, as grandparents we've grown enough in our personal faith to be able to assure our grandchildren and others of God's ultimate faithfulness.

It helps to remind ourselves of Isaiah 55:8: "'My thoughts are not your thoughts, neither are your ways my ways, declares the LORD.'" Our natural sight cannot see His supernatural working; it is in a different realm. Though God may at times seem silent, He is never at any time unhearing or unmoved by our need.

There is, however, one thing about prayer that's always instantaneous. It immediately covers any amount of miles or unseen circumstances. This is something those whose grandchildren are removed physically or emotionally gratefully count on. It's why Jan Young can now say of her once spiritually alienated daughter who now, along with her two granddaughters, lives many miles away: "She belongs to the Lord and I pray for her and her family daily."

Still, any grandparent who has ever lost track of his or her offspring for even a moment will understand the sudden anxiety of not seeing them or knowing what is happening in their lives. One such scary scenario is described by Kathy Macias.

A couple of years ago she and her husband treated their grown kids, spouses, and grandchildren to a day at Sea World near San Diego.

"Everyone was having a great time," Kathi says, "but as the day wore on, my 'grandma feet' got anxious to find a place to rest. While everyone else went to see yet another exhibit, my youngest son, Chris, and I opted to sit in the children's play area and relax while Chris's five-year-old son, Tyler, and his seven-year-old cousin, Chazz, ran off some excess energy."

Good plan—until Kathi suddenly realized they could no longer see the boys. In a split second, they seemed to have vanished into thin air.

"Stop everything!" Chris shouted. "My son is missing!" It was an illogical response, because, of course, the surrounding world wasn't about to stop. Yet when your offspring, the child of your heart, is out of sight, nothing else matters except knowing he or she is safe.

Seeing her son's face go pale, Kathi—though terrified, too—did the only thing she knew would immediately help. She began to pray. Doing so, she personally procured God's promise to protect. "They will call on me," states Psalm 91:15, "and I will answer them; I will be with them in trouble, I will deliver them and honor them."

God did honor Kathi's prayers. They soon found Tyler and Chazz, happily swimming in a shallow pool of freezing cold water under a waterfall.

"Being the devoted grandmother that I am," Kathi quips, "I immediately took the boys to a gift shop where I spent a month's salary on two matching Sea World sweat-suits. They were worth every penny."

Anyone alone in the dark with a mosquito knows it doesn't take a swarm to snap you out of a sound sleep. One of those little heat-seeking suckers whining in your ear will do it. Likewise, both long-distance grandparents and those whose children are spiritually lost understand how small concerns become magnified when we can't see what's happening. One mosquito-sized malady sends our imagination running wild. Soon fear has us sweating and swatting.

It's then we need to turn on the light, get on our knees, and spray—er, pray. Slather it on! Soon that fearful infestation swarming our psyche will be repelled by God's protective presence.

Sadly for some, it's not a matter of imagination. There's no doubt in our minds about the destruction taking place in our children and grandchildren's lives. As a result, many are purposely keeping us at arm's length. Despite our constant prayer coverage, some hellish horde is bent on destroying the harvest in our children's or grandchildren's lives. Lying in the sleepless dark, we wonder: *Have our prayers passed some invisible expiration date? What damage is being done in the meantime?*

That's when a bug blitz straight out of scripture may actually come as an encouragement. In Joel 2:25 God promises Israel that despite years of drought and destruction, "I will repay you for the years the locusts have eaten—the great locust and the young locust, the other locusts and the locust swarm."

Surely we've all heard testimonies from those whose lives were set on destruction yet were miraculously rescued and restored by their Maker. They're here, reminding us that God is still in the rebuilding business. If you would like to read a few of these renovation stories, pick up Jan Coleman's book *After the Locusts*.[1] In the meantime, remember this: throughout Scripture, God's had a lot of practice with plagues, and His Son was a carpenter. Both are eternal experts when it comes to de-bugging and rebuilding.

Still need help with that diabolical buzzing in your brain? Something that has helped me many times is to replace those swarming negative seductions with God's positive promises. "Finally, brothers," the apostle Paul writes to the Philippians, "whatever is true, whatever is noble, whatever is right, whatever is pure, whatever is lovely, whatever is admirable—if anything is excellent or praiseworthy—think about such things. Whatever you have learned or received or heard from me, or seen in me—put it into practice. And the God of peace will be with you" (Philippians 4:8-9). God's promises are like Calamine lotion for our bug-bitten emotions.

Speaking of bugs reminds me of the summer visit to my parents' when Derek discovered cicadas. These are large locust-looking bugs whose larvae burrow in the ground, then crawl out later and attach themselves to trees in order to hatch. Afterward, they leave behind a skeletal shell. Meanwhile, at twilight they make quite a resonating racket. The song of the cicada is, in fact, a favorite sound effect used by filmmakers to represent the fall of evening in the great outdoors.

Though cicadas are benign, non-biting bugs, Derek didn't know that. Hearing that kind of commotion and seeing the shells sent him quickly streaking for the safety of Grandma's house.

I have similar memories of sitting at night on an old porch swing located safely inside my maternal grandmother's screened-in front porch. It was a place I knew no bugs—or bogeymen—could get me.

Without question, a praying grandparent provides a special spiritual covering. Here is a great story Martha Bolton's middle son recently reminded her of.

"My husband's mother, Betty, used to come and stay with us for weeks at a time," Martha says. Since this son had a set of bunk beds, Grandma slept in his room on the bottom bunk."

One night, from the top, he called to her, "Grandma, I'm cold. Can you get me a blanket?"

Obligingly, Grandma got up and put a blanket over him.

No sooner had she climbed back into bed, than he called again, "Grandma, I'm still cold. Can you get me another blanket?"

So she did.

She had barely settled in when, sure enough, the kid repeated his request.

Undoubtedly a tad tired by now, Grandma threw on a third blanket.

No sooner had her head hit the pillow than these words wafted down: "Grandma, I'm hot now. Can you take one off?"

Without complaint, Grandma complied.

Martha's son tells how afterward he just lay there thinking, *Wow—my grandma really, really loves me!*

"Surely," Martha says, "she could have told him to get it himself or convinced him he didn't need all those blankets, but what kind of lasting impression would that memory have made?"

Here's the real topper. "Grandma Betty didn't have a lot to offer in the way of material things, but she prayed every day for our sons." Though Martha's son is now a grown man and Grandma has been gone for many years, he still remembers how she lovingly covered him, not just with blankets but with her prayers.

Such a feeling of safety and security comes with the knowledge of a grandparents' protective prayer. It's a gift that should never be taken for granted. One of the things that struck me hardest after first my grandmother then my mother passed away was how our family would no longer be able to count on that faithful covering.

For that very reason, let's take a lesson from Grandma Betty while we have the chance. No matter the hour or the inconvenience, keep piling the prayers on our children and grandchildren. At the same time, let's never miss the opportunity of encouraging them to pray so that, even when we're gone, we'll know God's got them covered.

CAMP GRAMMA CLIPBOARD #10

Looking for some new prayers to teach your grandchildren? Here are a couple of good Web sites you might want to check out:

- <www.indianchild.com/prayers_for_children.htm>
- <www.prayerguide.org.uk/prayerskids.htm>
- On one of them I found this little prayer that can easily be sung to the tune of "Taps." Have them imagine a trumpet being played at sunset, creating a simple, quieting way to end the day.

    Day is done
    Gone the sun
    From the lake,
    From the hills,
    From the sky.
    All is well; safely rest.
    God is nigh.

- Speaking of special bedtime prayers, here's some "toad-ally" practical advice from pastor's wife Susi Huson. Seems five-year-old grandson Judah has been struggling with fear as he goes to bed at night and often calls Grandma Susi for prayer before he goes to sleep. One day Judah came to visit, and his uncle presented him with a fat toad he had found in an outdoor woodpile. Typical boy, Judah was thrilled. He pulled its legs, tried to drown it, even chased Grandma with it. But as night and the trip home drew near, Judah's familiar bedtime fears surfaced, so before leaving he approached Grandma with his customary prayer request—except there on his shoulder was the toad, also in need of prayer. Good grandma that she is, Susi prayed for both. "Needless to say," she admits, "I kept one eye open!"

11
Breaking Camp

> *Go through the camp and tell the people,*
> *Get your supplies ready.*
> —Joshua 1:11

It was the last evening of our second Camp Gramma when someone noticed then ten-year-old grandson, Fallon, was missing. That was our majorly fun "Summer of the Monkeys" year. Now, like all good things, our time together was coming to an end. The Idaho kids' other grandma, Lynn, had come to collect them so they could all fly home together the next day, and we were standing at the door exchanging hugs, kisses, and final goodbyes. That's when someone said, "Where's Fallon?" A search through the house turned up nothing, so my husband headed for the backyard. There he found the boy face down on the ground crying his eyes out. Fallon didn't want Camp Gramma to end.

Hugging him tenderly to his heart, Grandpa assured him that we would see each other again soon and that more great times lay ahead. Still, he was inconsolable. Not knowing what else to do, we convinced Lynn to let the kids stay one more night with the promise of delivering them early the next morning. Quite honestly, we didn't want Camp Gramma to end either.

Though I didn't want to dwell on it, that heart-tugging episode brought me face-to-face with reality. How many years could Camp Gramma go on? Kids grow fast. Soon they would all be developing different interests and making critical choices that would undoubtedly take them in other directions.

What I especially didn't want to reflect long on is that Grandpa and I aren't getting any younger, either. Though I've determined to do family gatherings in some form or fashion as long as I can move, the reality is that we won't be around forever. Call me selfish, but I'm hoping when that happens they'll miss us for more than just our money.

This, of course, presents an even more serious issue. How do we prepare for the eventual day when Grandma and Grandpa take that last big one-way hike to heaven, breaking earthly camp forever? Yet isn't that what Camp Gramma is all about? Preparing our grandchildren while we're together for the inevitable times when we're apart, whether here or in eternity.

Either way, as Christians we know it's just a temporary parting. In the words of poet Emily Dickinson:

> *This world is not conclusion;*
> *A sequel stands beyond,*
> *Invisible, as music,*
> *But positive, as sound.*

Still, it never makes saying goodbye any easier. All the more reason we should make every moment count, pouring as much as we can into their lives as long as possible.

Lest this become morose, here's a humorous story recently shared by my ministry colleague Laurie Jacobs. Seems her friend, Fran, was discussing with her daughter the recent demise of an older family acquaintance. Sitting at the table taking in every detail was Fran's young grandson, Tavian. With each word his eyes widened as he realized the deceased was someone he knew. Someone's grandma! That's when the wheels in his head started turning. *Could that mean my grandma might die, too?* There was no time to waste.

"Grandma," Tavian blurted, "hold out your hands."

Surprised, Grandma did what her grandson asked. Taking both her hands in his small smooth ones, he closed his eyes, bowed his head, and prayed with preacher-like authority: "In Jesus' name, Grandma, I bless you with everlasting life!"

To his way of thinking, this was a situation requiring straight-to-the-point prayer. The good news is that because his grandma loves Jesus, she *will* live forever—just not here.

Still, by God's grace and the miracles of modern medicine, the little guy probably has no immediate worries. If Ann Gibson is any example, these days most grandparents' earthly tent strings stretch a lot farther than we might expect. Ann's been doing her Cousins' Camp for 12 years, during which time she's made some interesting observations.

"At the time we began, none of our children lived near us," says Ann. "Our original intent was to spend time with our grandchildren so we would be a part of their lives. What we found was that this yearly event is not only about us but also about the kids getting to know each other and keeping in contact."

Even so, Ann admits that as the children grow and mature, the year-to-year dynamic changes. "Sometimes for the better, sometimes for the worse," she says, "in the sense that the interests, skills, talents, and so on are not always as compatible as they once were. This makes each ensuing experience a challenge."

One way Ann has kept the older children involved as they began to "age out" of the typical camp activities was by using them to help plan and direct. Seems it's created an ageless connection. Her two oldest grandsons are now both college-age and working. Though they no longer participate in camp, they still try to be there on opening day for the camp bag distribution and a family meal.

Occasionally, though, someone has to miss. Last summer, the only week Ann's family could get everyone together eliminated their 13-year-old granddaughter, who had been accepted at an exclusive music camp—an opportunity everyone agreed she shouldn't miss, even for Cousins' Camp. "It was the right choice," Ann says, "but we're hoping to have her back next summer."

This tells us all a few important things, both earthly and eternal. First, especially for families who live far apart, an at-least-once-a-year reunion is the ideal for getting acquainted and staying connected. Whatever time we're able to arrange, the purpose is to make memories that will keep us alive forever in their hearts.

Next, getting the cousins connected builds bonds and strengthens ongoing family ties, providing opportunities for them to observe inherited similarities while also discovering their differences. Isn't that what being part of a family is all about? We can only hope this encourages them as the next generation to keep important family get-togethers and traditions going.

Last but not least, this may be our greatest ongoing opportunity to steer them toward making their own lifetime commitments to Christ. This not only assures them of a better life here but assures all of us a life together in the hereafter.

"Every year," Ann concedes, "there are challenges and changes. For instance, we now have several grandchildren on various kinds of medication. A few times sickness, triple-digit outdoor temperatures, even an inferior camping spot caused us to cancel. The big key is flexibility. Make a good plan, but don't be married to it."

Certainly today's unpredictable lifestyles give us all more incentive to induct our little campers at the earliest age feasible. The longer we can keep them under our influence, the more opportunities we have to show them how to set and follow their heavenly compasses.

Ann has no doubt realized how much Cousins' Camp has added to everyone getting acquainted. "Trying though it may become, it has been worth the time and effort over the years."

To me, no effort is too great to keep Camp Gramma going. That's why when now, nearly 14-year-old Fallon, who hates to fly, suggested last year that we take Camp Gramma "on the road," I immediately jumped on board. This culminated in my renting a small cabin near downtown Coeur D'Alene and transporting the entire Sacramento contingent, plus correlating equipment, to Idaho. That year's theme was "Summer of the Spies," which meant I had long been collecting all sorts of sleuthing stuff, including a more extensive Bible study that encouraged the kids to search the Scriptures for life-changing "clues." For me, it was our best time together yet. Toward the end, I decided to do a little sleuthing of my own to see if the grands felt the same.

"You know, kids," I started my investigation, "you're all growing up. Don't you think maybe you'll soon be too old for Camp Gramma?"

Their outcry could be heard for blocks around. "Too old for Camp Gramma? *No way!* We want to do this FOR-EV-ER."

Forever, of course, carries some far-reaching connotations. Still, this was exactly what I wanted to hear; and it was obviously true. Though now four years older, still-super-sensitive grandson Fallon cried at the end of that Camp Gramma, too.

So did Gramma.

Regardless of their current enthusiastic support, I realize every year brings us closer to the time when they'll all be grown and following their own futures. Even as I write this, the three oldest are showing the inevitable signs of teenage hormonal havoc.

Mentioning these mixed emotions brings up another inescapable fact: when you love people, tears come with the territory. Our middle son, Derek, was 12 years old when my mother was diagnosed with an extremely debilitating form of Parkinson's disease—one that rapidly resulted in dementia eventually robbing her of the ability to move or communicate. As her condition deteriorated, we quickly planned a family trip from California to my parents' home in Kansas. Derek's rendition of that last visit recently had us both bawling.

"Our time there was both sad and somewhat awkward," Derek remembers, "seeing Grandpa's frustration at trying to translate for her as the sickness began to affect her speech and watching the hope fading from her own eyes."

His dominating memory, though, was the day we left as she stood on the cement steps outside their home with tears streaming down her face, simply repeating "I love you, I love you . . ."

Derek said he knew then what she must have known the entire visit. That would be the last time we would all be together in this place. Even sadder, it would be the final time she would be able to say with words how much she loved us.

"It absolutely broke my heart," he said.

Not long after, we moved my parents to California so Dad could stay with us while Mom spent her remaining two years in a full-time care facility. He bunked with our youngest son, Dustin, and the two of them became very close—so much that on the night before my mother died, Dustin had a dream in which he saw Grandpa sitting with his head bowed in his hands. "When I woke up," Dustin told me later, "I already knew what had happened."

It's inescapable. Life's tapestry will have some dark threads woven among the rest. Yet there's no doubt that going through tough times as a family brings us all closer. As sure as the happy times weave us together with ribbons of laughter and love, the tearful times tie an unbreakable knot, binding us forever heart-to-heart.

So when the question arises, "Should we try to shield our grandchildren from life's natural consequences and inevitable sorrows?" my answer is "No." Rather, I believe we should use every opportunity to model for them the importance of living each day on earth to its fullest, loving each other unabashedly, and sharing our Christian hope of being together forever with Jesus in eternity.

This also means never missing the chance to tell or show others how much we love them.

Jan Coleman remembers the day in college when the phone rang in her dorm. On the other end of the line was her father's shaky voice. "Your Grandma Hallie has passed on." Tearfully Jan hung up the phone.

"I hadn't visited her in months," Jan recalls, "because I couldn't bear to see her failing away in the nursing home. I was filled with guilt that I hadn't the courage to be there, to tell her how much I loved her."

Surely we all have similar regrets. One of our biggest modern-day nemeses is being so busy that we sometimes take for granted the things and people that are most important. Only when they're gone do we realize how much more might have been said or done. Perhaps this presents the most critical case for being intentional about planning frequent times together.

This quote from author Max Lucado puts it all in perspective: "When you are in the final days of your life, what will you want? Will you hug that college degree in the walnut frame? Will you ask to be carried to the garage so you can sit in your car? Will you find comfort in rereading your financial statement? Of course not. What will matter then will be people. If relationships will matter most then, shouldn't they matter most now?"

Two touching testimonies illustrating both our earthly impact and heavenly hope come from people we've met in previous chapters. Nettie Lankford describes her grandma as a short, overweight lady with gray hair done up in a little bun on the back of her head who wore glasses and funny laced-up shoes.

"She may not have looked like a lot to the world," says Nettie, "but anyone who looked into her eyes saw Jesus. I will always cherish the times I spent with her and the things she taught me about living for God. She was the greatest lady I have ever known. Grandma went to be with the Lord in May 1963, and I think it was the saddest day of my life. However, I know someday I will see her again in heaven."

Star Richardson also attests to both of her grandmothers being incredible women of faith and the two most special people in her life. "I can't wait to see them in heaven and hug their necks," Star told me through her tears. "I'm sure they'll be right next to Jesus!"

The most important thing is assuring our grandchildren that whatever happens on earth, it's not the end. As Christians, we are headed for heaven and cherish the hope of seeing them there one day. This, of course, requires that they also accept Christ and commit their lives to following Him.

So how do we positively broach these sensitive life-and-death subjects with our grandchildren? In an online devotional, Kathi Macias once wrote about taking her then preschool-age granddaughter with her to deliver some flowers at the cemetery:

> My granddaughter was naturally curious about what sort of place a "sembletery" was, so I did my best to explain. As we read a few headstones, I told her what the dates meant, and we figured the ages of a few of the deceased. Then we came to one where a woman had died at 102.
>
> "Wow!" my granddaughter exclaimed, her brown eyes widening in awe. "She was ready!"
>
> Needless to say, I had a good chuckle over that. But it also gave me an opportunity to talk with Brittney about what "being ready" really meant and about the way people will remember us once we're gone.

Age, of course, is a catchy concept for children. To them every adult seems old. To us it's all relative; the older we get, the younger *old* becomes. Consequently, we would do especially well to draw their attention to the small dash carved between the birth and death dates, using it as an illustration—not to mention a personal reminder—that in the end, what matters most is not when we enter and depart life, but what we accomplish during the dash in between. It was Dutch Holocaust survivor and author Corrie ten Boom who said, "The measure of a life, after all, is not its duration, but its donation."

By the way, according to a quote from the late playwright A. W. Pinero, living and loving each moment to its fullest has a definite impact on aging. "Those who love deeply never grow old" he states. "They may die of old age, but they die young." One can only hope that the 102-year-old woman's long life was full of the kind of love and happiness that kept her heels kicking up to the end.

One warning: once the subject is broached, we should be prepared for probable questions about what happens to those who die without accepting Christ. Surely the Bible is plain about the dire consequences of this circumstance (Romans 6:23; Revelation 20:14-15). Thankfully, though, it has much more to say about God's grace and the provision made for those who accept it. Likewise, while it's important that we always be truthful with our grandchildren, we can do so without making harsh judgments, providing more information than they can digest, or dwelling on the negative. Rather, let's emphasize the good news of God's love and grace, the importance of embracing it, and sharing our faith with others.

Kids, in fact, can be some of the best evangelists ever—something those of us who are still praying for unbelieving friends and family might be encouraged to remember. In their guileless honesty and enthusiasm, children's words often find a way to penetrate the hardest hearts. Take for instance the little boy who proudly announced one day that he knew exactly what the Bible meant. Sure enough, when asked to explain, his answer inarguably summed it all up: "It's <u>B</u>asic <u>I</u>nformation <u>B</u>efore <u>L</u>eaving <u>E</u>arth."

Every seasoned camper knows that before breaking camp, it's good to take time for two things: reflecting on the time spent together and lessons learned, then making a final check of the grounds. Likewise in life, we should emphasize to our grandchildren the benefits of assessing and embracing each experience, keeping only what's worthwhile, and trashing the rest.

In the Old Testament book of Joshua, God gives some similar instruction. For years Joshua had been Moses' main sidekick. Now that had all changed. In Joshua 1:1-3, the Almighty, as usual, minces no words: "The LORD said to Joshua, son of Nun, Moses' aide, 'Moses my servant is dead. Now then, you and all these people, get ready to cross the Jordan River into the land I am about to give to them.'"

This scripture stresses two very important things: First, no matter how well-loved or how important their individual contributions, people come and go. Second, those who remain must move on. Breaking camp is necessary if we are to experience greater adventures, win bigger battles, and learn larger lessons.

Verse 11 indicates these were realities Joshua had little choice but to capture quickly. "So Joshua ordered the officers of the people, 'Go through the camp and tell the people, Get your supplies ready.'"

No small task, I imagine. After 40 years of wilderness wandering, the children of Israel had surely accumulated some serious stuff. Likewise, if your grandchildren are like mine, it doesn't take 40 minutes following arrival for them to pull out everything they've packed. By the time camp ends—thanks to Grandma—they've accumulated a lot more. This means at some point we must do some major sorting, helping them repack what's most important for the journey home.

Inevitably some of the tinier trinkets they've collected get lost even before they leave. A few will be found later, wedged between couch cushions or stuck in strands of carpet—sentimental discoveries that always find me filling a tissue or two. Even the intangible left-behinds can bring tears. I remember my mother telling me how hard it was for her to wipe my boys' little handprints off the windows after we left.

The same is true spiritually. We can only pray the grands, too, will make a few future discoveries, finding the intangible things we've tucked into their hearts during our time together; that our lessons, encouragement, and love are things they'll carry with them long after the loot is lost.

Now for one last illustration from the Israelites. The land they were about to enter was called Canaan—the Promised Land. Promised or not, it was a place they had never been. Though God had previously made both His intention and ability to part the waters plain, seems they still needed reassurance before jumping the Jordan. Could that be why God sent the priests across first?

"So when the people broke camp to cross the Jordan," reads Joshua 3:15, "the priests carrying the ark of the covenant went ahead of them."

This ark was not the Noah kind, rather a gilded box holding the Ten Commandments, Aaron's rod, and some manna—all symbols of God's spiritual guidelines, earthly leadership, and heavenly provision. Still, I suppose God could have miraculously floated it across. Instead, He chose to have the priests carry it. Why? God knows we flesh-and-blood humans need someone likewise clothed to pave the pathway.

In a much greater sense, that's why He sent Jesus. Not only to pave the way to heaven, but so we could see God in human form and more easily accept what He had been trying to tell us for centuries. "The word became flesh," states John 1:14, "and made his dwelling among us."

Thirty-three years later, when the time came for Jesus to head back to heaven, He, too, began the process of preparing His disciples. In John 14:1-4, Jesus comforts their concerns by describing the many rooms in His Father's house. "I am going there," He promises, "to prepare a place for you."

Ever notice how much it helps when facing an unfamiliar journey to know that someone has not only scouted the way before us but waits at the other end in a cozy bed and breakfast? In that same comforting sense, some of us must go ahead to heaven and form a greeting party. Meanwhile, let's make the Promised Land so appealing to our loved ones that they'll want to meet us there.

Fact is, I would like to believe that every mansion has its own celestial campground. Think of it—Jesus and generations of friends and family will be waiting. Why, heaven could be the greatest Camp Gramma ever! Some will be people we've never even known on earth, meaning my grands will get to meet the likes of my Grandma Witt. Imagine the fun to find her dancing around the campfire, even as she purportedly did a Spirit-inspired jig around the old wood-burning stove warming her little country church. Suddenly it seems clear why one of my dad's favorite old hymns was one titled "I Won't Have to Cross Jordan Alone."

Another hillbilly hymn my family sometimes sang was one titled "Will the Circle Be Unbroken?" It sets to music the plaintive question of whether or not our earthly family will be eternally intact. For those of us struggling today with the same concern, perhaps it will help to be reminded that, because of sin, the Israelites, too, wandered the wilderness 40 years before finally coming to rest in the Promised Land. Undeniably, some were lost long the way. The good news is that God's presence never left them. Day and night, His love and care surrounded them.

Likewise, we must believe that long after we're gone, God will continue His attempts at directing those we love, keeping the lessons we've left in their hearts constantly before them.

Undoubtedly someone is just now thinking, *But what if God calls me home while their salvation still seems uncertain?* Perhaps these words from author Victor Hugo will lend you hope: "Have courage for the great sorrows of life and patience for the small ones; and when you have laboriously accomplished your daily tasks, go to sleep in peace. God is awake." Or as Psalm 121:4 puts it, "Indeed, he who watches over Israel [His loved ones] will neither slumber nor sleep."

Face it—some things we may simply never know. Yet, as a friend once said, "We'll undoubtedly be more surprised by who makes it to heaven than who does not." Whatever the eternal outcome, God promises that no tears will ruin the celestial celebration with those who eventually arrive.

A few years ago, my husband and I were waiting to board a plane when behind us there was quite a commotion. Even before I could turn to see, an energetic young boy streaked past pulling a frazzled flight attendant by the hand. An identification tag flopping around his neck indicated that the lad was flying alone, the lady obviously assigned to get him safely on the plane.

Jim and I gave each other "the look," meaning our typical luck would have us seated somewhere near the little loudmouth. Sure enough, he ended up catty-cornered across the aisle. Next to him—God bless her—was a sweet lady who took him under her wing and struck up a conversation. Thanks to his high-pitched voice, the entire plane soon knew two things: this was his first flight, and he was headed to visit Grandma. Admittedly, his adolescent excitement was contagious.

As the plane pulled back from the gate, his nonstop questions started. "Are we taking off?" "How long will it be?" "Is it scary?" Taxiing down the runway, the patient lady assured him she would point out the exact moment the plane left the ground. When that time finally came, the boy's arm suddenly shot straight up in the air.

"I'm comin', Gramma!" he hollered.

Everyone aboard the plane burst into laughter.

Without a doubt, somewhere out there a loving grandma was waiting for this energetic little elf to arrive. How heartwarming to think that one day we, too, will be watching from heaven, listening for those very same words.

CAMP GRAMMA CLIPBOARD #11

Looking for positive ways to broach the subject of life and death with your grandchildren?

- Consider taking them, as Kathi Macias did, on their own trip to the "sembletary." Not only do children have a natural curiosity about these things, but they can often be quite matter-of-fact about them. Therefore, a "sembletary" visit might provide a proactive, non-emotional means of emphasizing to our grandchildren how every person on earth has only a set amount of time.
- While there, offer a supporting scripture or two. There is "a time to be born and a time to die," the writer of Ecclesiastes 3:2 tells us, while the Psalmist assures: "My times are in your hands" (Psalm 31:15).
- Whatever the discussion, make sure they see heaven as a real and positive place.
- Having pets that die—whether yours or someone else's—also provides an opportunity to talk about what happens afterward. I'll never forget when my boys' first dog was hit by a car. We had just left his furry little body at the humane society for disposal and were all sitting in the car blubbering. "Never be ashamed to show emotion over someone you love," I told them, wanting to be sure they understood that grieving death is a necessary and important part of life.

12
Roots and Wings

*Remember those who led you, who spoke the word of God to you;
and considering the result of their conduct, imitate their faith.*
—Hebrews 13:7, NASB

"I am an oil heiress," Peggy Musgrove's friend Edith proudly announced to her one day. The twinkle in Edith's eye should have clued Peggy in, but instead she took her seriously.

"Really? Tell me about it."

Evidently Edith's brother had uncovered some papers showing that their father retained mineral rights to the family farm in Oklahoma. Knowing the richness of the oil pools in that state, he had investigated the claim's current validity. Sure enough, the rights were still in their father's name, and his heirs would receive the benefits.

Smiling, Edith showed Peggy her first annual check—the smashing sum of $2.31. Hardly an earthly inheritance, much less a lasting legacy, it did buy them both a good laugh.

Likewise, as grandparents, the time comes when we must consider what we've been bequeathed and the legacy we'll leave behind, monetarily and otherwise. Had Edith's inheritance been many times multiplied, some might have deemed her rich and her heirs most fortunate. Yet material wealth, measured in the currency of the culture, carries only its immediate value. This can change quickly with the whimsical winds of man's vacillating economic system. Ask anyone caught in America's current economic crisis. That's why spiritual stakes are more important than earthly stocks. As one friend summed up her grandmother's spiritual legacy, "It doesn't include a financial windfall, but a spiritual updraft."

Southern journalist William Hodding Carter II says it this way: "There are only two lasting bequests we can hope to give our children. One of these is roots; the other, wings."

Over the years others have elaborated on his well-known quote. Jonas Salk, for instance, described these roots as "symbolic of home" while the wings were for "flying away and exercising what's been taught." Author Denis Waitley calls them "roots of responsibility and wings of independence." Another online advisor told a first-time father that roots "keep kids grounded through tough times while wings allow them to soar."

While those are all good and true, to me none quite captures the spiritual significance. As this book has attempted to illustrate, that's where Christian grandparents play an integral part. Putting down spiritual stakes in our children's and grandchildren's lives also provides both roots and wings, only in a divinely deeper and heavenly higher sense.

Certainly as it pertains to earthly roots, we have the history to help our grandchildren better understand where their looks, personalities, and characteristics came from. This can be especially important during the tumultuous teenage transition when kids commonly question everything. Hopefully we can bridge that gap by sharing significant snippets of past history that cause them to feel more comfortable in their own skin. At the same time, we should celebrate their uniqueness, encouraging them to embrace it too.

Truth be told, it can take us all a while to settle into ourselves. As Calvin Thielman so poignantly put it, "The older you get, the more like yourself you become." Even if that means you're also a lot like someone else.

Take our son Derek. Looks-wise, he is, as some grassroots ancestor might say, the "spittin' image" of his late Grandpa Braddy. This is something he's been told often, causing him to be curious.

"Grandpa Braddy passed before I was born," he recently wrote, "so I know the least about him; yet, for me, he has always been intriguing. My whole life I've been compared to him in appearance and sometimes demeanor. I wonder. Do we share the same introspection, competitive fire, vices, and veils? Seeing the reverent respect with which my father remembers him makes me ponder what I might have learned from his presence."

If Derek will continue listening to and observing his dad, he can still learn a lot about his grandfather and himself. Not only did Dad, too, inherit similar looks but also many of his father's outstanding attributes.

Then there's our hat heritage. Why else would Dustin always wear his baseball hat up and off to the side of his head just like my dad did? Or Damon and Derek, when they were small, refuse to go hatless, even hanging them on their bedposts at night so they could plop them on first thing in the morning? Though they don't remember, rarely did either grandpa go anywhere without a hat. Even today, when the Braddy boys go out, the hats go on.

As author Gail Buckley put it, "Family faces are magic mirrors. Looking at people who belong to us, we see the past, present, and future." Undoubtedly that's why those who are adopted often develop an itch later in life to find their birth parents. Good or bad, there's something about seeing where we came from that gives us a greater insight into our identity. For many, this reunion provides an otherwise unreachable lever, releasing them to move on.

In some cases, of course, finding family isn't feasible. Then having those who love and accept us no matter what becomes all the more important.

Two of Connie Clements' grandchildren are adopted. Connie is white, and both adopted grandchildren are African-American. One came to them at five weeks old, the other at seven weeks. When grandson Spencer, cousin to the adopted ones, was waiting for his mommy to deliver his second brother, he and Grandma were at the house getting some rest. Following Spencer's nap, they were snuggling and talking.

"Grandma," Spencer asked out of the blue, "do you think baby Sam is going to be brown or white?" Since they have both colors in their family, he simply assumed babies come out randomly. Most refreshing is that to him it obviously made no difference.

No sooner had Spencer solved the adoption dilemma than younger brother, Jack, took a turn with confusion. His question arose when Jack saw Grandma Connie holding someone else's brand-new baby at church.

"Grandma," he whispered in her ear, "is that another one of our cousins?"

Again, given the circumstances, why should he be surprised if someone new suddenly showed up? The deeper root issue is this. Thanks to some good grandparenting, both brothers were ready and willing to accept any and all new additions.

Even under common circumstances, life can be confusing. Haven't all of us found ourselves wondering at times, *Where in the world did that idea, attribute, or interest come from?* Much that is handed down, recorded or unrecorded, has an uncanny way of popping up on the pages of our lives at the most unexpected moments. Like seeds in spring, it's sometimes surprising what works its way to the surface.

Not to bum you out, but this brings us all back full-circle to the age issue. The inescapable fact is that being grandparents means many of us are old enough to know how our grandparents' and parents' stories ended. Throughout the book, I've shared some of those glimpses, both mine and others.

Our stories, our children's, and grandchildren's, however, are still being written. Undoubtedly we all harbor hopes about how these epics will end. Yet, as an author, I've learned something: a lot can happen in the writing and editing process to affect and change that. That's why understanding how just one affirming word from us can alter another's course and outcome is so important. Many are the testimonies of those directly attributing their faith to a beloved grandparent who faithfully shared God's good news.

Even more surprising to some, we are actually all sequels. According to Hebrews 11:39-12:3, not only does each succeeding Christian generation contribute spiritually to the accomplishments of the last, but many who've gone on to heaven are waiting to receive their reward based on what we do. "These were all commended for their faith," reads Hebrews 11:39-40, "yet none of them received what had been promised. God had planned something better for us, so that only together with us would they be made perfect."

Wow. Kinda places our grandparenting role in a whole new dimension, doesn't it? The real ongoing good news is that we have this great privilege, as long as God gives us breath, of contributing to these wonderful works through our children and grandchildren. Our greatest prayer is that each of our lives will have a spiritually happy ending so we can all have a happy heavenly beginning. That's why everything that's said and done must point to the ultimate Author. "Let us fix our eyes on Jesus," Hebrews 12:2 tells us, "the author and perfecter of our faith."

In the meantime, we get to enjoy editing our precious prodigies' own chapters of earthly history. Despite the nay-sayers and scary world circumstances, I believe with God's help our grandchildren have amazing opportunities to impact society. Thanks to technology, they may do more in their lifetimes than we ever hoped or dreamed, not just imitating our faith but taking it to a whole new level. A big part of this is inspiring the development of their God-given gifts and abilities.

Jan Coleman's grandmother was an aspiring writer who dabbled mostly with short stories and letters to the editor. Seeing Jan's own passion for writing, she encouraged her to pursue it. She then bequeathed Jan the cardboard box filled with her unpublished stories and newspaper articles. Though it would be many years and devastating family detours later before Jan finally fulfilled her lifelong dream of becoming a published author, she always knew it was because of her grandmother's encouragement and inspiration.

Here's Jan's read on the roots-and-wings issue: "While it's true that family traditions give children identity, godly wisdom is what gives them the ability to rise above adversity. This is one of the most powerful and loving gifts we can leave behind."

Along those lines, let me insert this thought. Certainly not all of us have the interest in or talent for leaving a writing legacy. Or do we? As I always tell those in my writing workshops, there are reasons to write more important than being published. If we don't take time to write things down, many family stories and much history may be lost.

Perhaps you procrastinate, thinking your stories aren't that interesting or important. That's what Jan's grandma thought. "There's nothing exciting about me," she told Jan, "but here are my scribblings."

Nothing exciting? It was as Jan read these "scribblings" that she learned how her grandmother had survived the great San Francisco earthquake as a toddler, struggled as a young married through the Great Depression, and sent her only son off to war. Most important, every story was laced with her deep faith in God and His ways.

"Her stories became a link across generations, a window to her soul," Jan says. "They were tales of life woven from her perspective, her passion, and her prayers. I read them often, not only to know her better but also to understand my own roots of faith."

Think about it. Through her grandmother's writings, Jan received both roots and wings. She'll tell you today that from them came her grandmother's most important life lesson: God is more interested in our character than our accomplishments.

Famous early-1900s theologian Charles Spurgeon agrees. "A good character is the best tombstone," he said. "Those who loved you, and were helped by you, will remember you when forget-me-nots are withered. Carve your name on hearts, and not on marble."

To Jan, her grandmother's life modeled Matthew 6:19-21: "Do not store up for yourselves treasures on earth, where moth and rust destroy, and where thieves break in and steal. But store up for yourselves treasures in heaven.... For where your treasure is, there your heart will be also."

Talking treasure reminds me of the year we chose "Summer of the Pirates" as our Camp Gramma theme. Since this included a two-day adventure to San Francisco, a boat tour of Alcatraz Island, and side trip to the famous Monterey Bay Aquarium, the moms and dads weren't about to miss it. Even with fourteen landlubbers in tow, it was a whale of a good time. Only once did I consider throwing someone overboard.

Perhaps you, too, have a motley crew like mine. If so, it may help to remember that of all our earthly possessions, our children and grandchildren are the only things we can take to heaven with us. Our families are the greatest gift God gives us. That's why we must treasure and teach them well, making sure they know that on the map to heaven the only cross that really marks the spot is the one Jesus died on.

Here's another nugget of truth. In the end it won't matter to our grandchildren how accomplished or well-known we were to the world. This was something James Bridges learned one day as he showed his grandson through his office. Seeing all the plaques and paraphernalia denoting his grandpa's high denominational position caused the boy's curiosity to surface. "Grandpa, someone told me you are an important man. Is that true?"

"No," Reverend Bridges humbly and wisely responded, "I'm just your grandpa."

In obvious relief, and to Grandpa's great delight, the boy replied, "That's what I thought!"

Truly that was all that really mattered. And he was right. "The most important work you and I will ever do," stated Harold B. Lee, "will be within the walls of our own homes."

So ask yourself these questions. "What personal ability might I share with my grandchildren? What special gift or interest have I observed them exhibiting?" Whether it's teaching what we know or paying for lessons, let's encourage them in whatever way we are able, while we are able.

Judging from something my friend Teri Herndon recently told me, that could be longer than we think. Seems her 91-year-old grandma is planning to attend her great-grandson's graduation from the same Bible college she attended. Now that's a far-reaching, long-teaching legacy, both earthly and spiritually.

Conversely, the saddest epitaph ever written is that of an influential person who loses his or her spiritual moorings. While researching her family's far-reaching roots, to her dismay Peggy Musgrove discovered this very scenario. Soon after their early-1700s arrival in America, her ancestors joined the Society of Friends—commonly called Quakers. Theirs was a strong faith that brought them through years of persecution, especially during the Revolutionary War—a direct result of their pacifistic beliefs. Then in the early 1800s, for some unknown reason, Peggy's paternal great-great-grandfather, John, left the church.

"From that point on," Peggy noted, "no succeeding family members were listed as having any church connection. Though faith had kept that side of the family together for almost one hundred years, in one generation it was lost. By leaving the church, great-great-Grandfather John made a decision not only for himself but for future descendants."

Why did Grandpa John leave the faith? Sadly, Peggy will never know. "What I do know," she states firmly, "is the value of passing my faith on to the next generation. I'll do everything I can to share what I learned from my mother and my other grandmother. I want my children and grandchildren to know the Lord."

Undoubtedly we've all known those who've fallen from faith, even in our own era. How well I remember the ecumenical exodus of the late 1960s when many of my own baby boom generation dumped religion, lumping it in with the materialistic establishment. Mostly it was a convenient excuse to do what they wanted. This resulted in raising some spiritually rootless offspring. No wonder the next Generation was simply dubbed "X." With so many missing their spiritual identity, no one knew what else to call them—leastwise themselves.

Perhaps this is why, as a retreat speaker, I now often find myself pointing people to Psalm 139, a powerfully poetic passage of Scripture assuring us that even when we've forgotten who we are, God always knows. It makes plain how He planned for and loved us before we were born. As Augustine once inferred, there truly is a God-shaped hole in every heart that only He can fill.

It also explains why, in the aftermath of America's terrorist attacks on September 11, 2001, many were seen not just walking but racing back to church. Instinctively they were looking for something they had either left behind or never knew—a Power high enough to not only help face the horror but also bring peace and order into their personal lives.

It's in just such unsettled times that the insight of a generation who hung in while others were bailing out is especially important. We are the carriers of not just a courageous Christian history but also a currently relevant reverence for God—both worthy of preserving and passing on. Not to be discounted are those new to faith but equally determined to instigate an ongoing family legacy. Either way, thank God for those who are passing on their spiritual heritage and reinforcing it in their children.

Which marches us right back to Camp Gramma.

When asked what spiritual impact her annual Cousins' Camp has had on her grandchildren, Ann Gibson said this: "Perhaps if our grands did not already come from strong Christian homes, there would be a more immediate noticeable impact. I do believe, though, that experiencing the legacy of a family of strong believers who try to live as Christians and follow the Bible's guidelines for faith and behavior will have a huge, long-term impact."

Ann notes that the older their grands get, the more they see how these observations are helping them in their own Christian walk. Two of their grandchildren have already requested to be baptized in water during Cousins' Camp and chose their "Papa" to do the honors. "Such great memories for all!" she concludes.

Memories. Isn't that what Camp Gramma is really all about? "Remember those who led you," Hebrews 13:7 says, "who spoke the word of God to you; and considering the result of their conduct, imitate their faith." May God grant that our children and grandchildren observe something in our lives that causes faith to take root in their own, then wing its way into the hearts of generations to come.

At a recent meeting, Connie Clements caught up with me to announce she had just had her annual Cousins' Camp. "The best one yet!" she proudly proclaimed. Guess one of her grands was already anticipating that. According to Connie, he told his mom the morning they were packing for camp, "Mom, this is the best day of my life!"

Now I ask you. What better endorsement on earth could there be? Or in heaven?

Long live Camp Gramma!

CAMP GRAMMA CLIPBOARD #12

Looking for ways to leave a lasting legacy?

- Consider doing what several contributing grandmas already mentioned. Start the tradition of compiling both family and event-oriented photo albums and scrapbooks, giving them as gifts at Christmas or some other special occasion. You can make them plain, fancy, or in between. Since scrapbooking has now become an all-out industry, the options for embellishing are endless. Don't forget, though, to collect free bits of memorabilia from every outing such as tickets, postcards, napkins, and so on. I've even used logos cut from gift shop bags.
- Collect old photos and make a generational album. Computer technology now makes it easier and less expensive than ever to scan, copy, and artistically arrange pictures. Looking through these albums together also provides an excellent opportunity to talk about heritage and emphasize the importance of carrying on traditions, Christian and otherwise.
- Compile, compose, and produce a professionally bound heritage book by looking online either for personal computer programs or companies specializing in helping you put them together. These usually include both pictures and text. According to Heritage Makers rep Linda Mendoza, it's "an amazing way to capture memories, preserve legacy and heritage, promote healing and happiness, and strengthen families, one storybook at a time."
- Take Peggy Musgrove's challenge to trace your family's genealogy and faith back to previous generations. Again, there are many online options and organizations that can help get you started.
- Finally and most spiritually important, ask yourself these two questions:

What if anything is hindering the transmission of my faith to the next generation?

What steps am I taking to intentionally pass that faith on?

- And in case you've somehow missed the entire point of this book—*consider starting your own Camp Gramma!*

Notes

Chapter 1
    1. Sharon Hoffman, *A Car Seat in My Convertible? Giving Your Grandkids the Spiritual Ride of Their Lives* (Birmingham, Ala.: New Hope Publishers, May 2008).
    2. Donna Otto, *The Gentle Art of Mentoring* (Eugene, Oreg.: Harvest House Publishers, 1995).

Chapter 4
    1. Rick Osborne and Ed Strauss, *Amazing and Unexplainable Things in the Bible* (Grand Rapids: Zonderkidz, 2004).
    2. Sam Huddleston, *Five Years to Life* (Springfield, Mo.: Onward Books, 2007).

Chapter 5
    1. Jan Karon, *Jan Karon's Mitford Cookbook and Reader* (New York: Viking, 2004).
    2. Judi Braddy, *Prodigal in the Parsonage* (Kansas City: Beacon Hill Press of Kansas City, 2004), 8.

Chapter 6
    1. John Draper, "Hitting 60 and Still Booming," *Christian Retailing*, September 18, 2006, 42.
    2. <www.youngeagles.org>.
    3. Tom McMahon, "Kid Tips," *Sacramento Bee,* July 28, 2006.

Chapter 7
    1. Heritage Makers, <www.mytreasuredkeepsakes.com>.
    2. Visit <www.webkinz.com> and click on the Webkinz search engine for a tour.
    3. Arlene Uslander, "Coping with Long-Distance Grandparenting," *Sierra Mountain Times,* August 17, 2007, 14.

Chapter 9
    1. <www.personalpromisebible.com>.

Chapter 10
    1. Jan Coleman, *After the Locusts* (Nashville: Broadman & Holman, 2002).

Navigate
the unexpected

With humor and refreshing honesty, author Judi Braddy shares the true north points she learned while living in Alaska and explains how these points have helped her keep her bearings—even through life's most battering storms.

True North
Staying on Course Through Life's Changing Circumstances
Judi Braddy
ISBN: 978-0-8341-2341-0

Available wherever books are sold

ALSO BY JUDI BRADDY

Prodigal in the Parsonage gives you, especially if you're in ministry, an insider's perspective and time-tested encouragement for struggling with trials that come when your child rejects faith.

Receive the insight and encouragement you need to endure the grief and anxiety of parenting a prodigal.

Prodigal in the Parsonage
Encouragement for Ministry Leaders Whose Child Rejects Faith
By Judi Braddy
ISBN: 978-0-8341-2206-2

Available wherever books are sold.

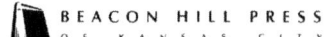

GIVE YOUR GRANDCHILDREN
A GIFT THEY'LL TREASURE FOR ETERNITY

Includes:
- Ideas for passing along a spiritual heritage to your grandchildren
- Guidance for maintaining good relationships with their parents
- Guidelines for establishing rules
- Ideas for developing a sense of family heritage and history

The Power of a Godly Grandparent
Leaving a Spiritual Legacy
By Stephen and Janet Bly

ISBN: 978-0-8341-2037-2

Available wherever Christian books are sold.

www.ingramcontent.com/pod-product-compliance
Lightning Source LLC
LaVergne TN
LVHW051519070426
835507LV00023B/3203